The Bra Book

The Fashion Formula to Finding the Perfect Bra

Jené Luciani

Illustrations by Ralph Voltz

BENBELLA BOOKS, INC.
DALLAS, TEXAS

All celebrity quotes (except Melissa Rivers') are from http://thinkexist.com/quotes/with/keyword/bra/.

Water Push-up Bra™, Dress & Lingerie Tapes™, American Sports Bra™, Breakthrough™, Double Dry™, 02Cool™, Sun Life™, Elements of Bliss™, BraBABY™, Scotch Tape™, and swoop and scoop™ are trademarked.

Fashion Forms®, Breast Petals®, Strap Tamers®, Strap-Mate®, Miracle Bra®, Maidenform®, Lycra®, Wonderbra®, Velcro®, Brava®, Spanx®, NuBra®, Coolmax®, PlayDry®, and Itty Bitty Bra® are all registered trademarks of their respective companies.

The photographs on pages 17 (right), 30 (left and top right), 34, and 36 are courtesy Fashion Forms. The photographs on pages 14, 16, and 168 are courtesy Fredrick's of Hollywood. The photograph on page 17 (left) is courtesy Wonderbra. The photographs on pages 30 (bottom right) and 31 are courtesy Shirley of Hollywood. The photographs on pages 33 and 96 are courtesy Amoena. The photographs on page 135 are courtesy Sassybax. The photograph on page 181 is courtesy Dirty Dolls Lingerie. The photograph on page 187 is courtesy Shapeez. The photograph on page 188 is courtesy The Little Bra Company. Rights to the following images were purchased from iStockphoto.com: page 48, ©iStockphoto.com/blaneyphoto; pages 79–80 (figure illustration), ©iStockphoto.com/SaulHerrera;

page 87, ©iStockphoto.com/DomenicoGelermo; page 90, ©iStockphoto.com/Joni_R; page 93, ©iStockphoto.com/webphotographeer; page 99, ©iStockphoto.com/jwebb; page 106, ©iStockphoto.com/mocker_bat; page 107, ©iStockphoto.com/YazolinoGirl; page 136, ©iStockphoto.com/cristi_m; page 137, ©iStockphoto.com/TACrafts.

BenBella Books, Inc.
6440 N. Central Expressway, Suite 503
Dallas, TX 75206
www.benbellabooks.com
Send feedback to feedback@benbellabooks.com

Printed in China
10 9 8 7 6 5 4 3 2 1

Library of Congress Cataloging-in-Publication Data is available for this title.

Proofreading by Erica Lovett and Stacia Seaman
Cover and text design and composition by Kit Sweeney
Printed by Wai Man Book Binding (China) Ltd

Distributed by Perseus Distribution
perseusdistribution.com

To place orders through Perseus Distribution:
Tel: 800-343-4499
Fax: 800-351-5073
E-mail: orderentry@perseusbooks.com

Significant discounts for bulk sales are available.
Please contact Glenn Yeffeth at glenn@benbellabooks.com or (214) 750-3628.

ACKNOWLEDGMENTS

Special thanks to my husband, Bill, who gave up months of seeing me (and dealt with piles of dishes in the sink) so I could constantly work on this book (and who listened to years, months, and days of endless bra talk).

Also special thanks to Ann Deal and the team at Fashion Forms for their unparalleled support, and bra designer extraordinaire Tara Cavosie for believing in this and helping to make it all happen.

Extra special thanks to Kristina Holmes and Michael Ebeling, my illustrious agents, for believing in me and this book and contributing their brilliant ideas (bras and all!) that helped to make it such a success, as well as the team at BenBella Books, especially Glenn Yeffeth, who was enthusiastic about this project from the start, and Leah Wilson, who deserves as much credit for this book as I do, and is now a "bra guru" in her own right.

To Janet C. Blake, the eagle-eyed copy editor who kept me on track (and prevented embarrassing comma splices and run-on sentences). To Judy Lederman, a fellow author and good friend who, when I said, "I could write a whole book on bras alone," responded with two words: "Do it."

To illustrator Ralph Voltz and designer Kit Sweeney, many thanks for beautifully bringing my words to life.

To supermodel Beverly Johnson, for sharing her story, and to all the women and men (especially pro-wrestler Brimstone!) I have interviewed in this book for being courageous enough to take part. To those of you who may have giggled about the subject matter, I hope you find the information contained within useful and informative (and while slightly humorous at times, not laugh-out-loud funny).

To my fellow journalists and members of the media, for your continued support, as well as Ann-Marie Nieves of Get Red PR; Jennifer Canzoneri, Adrienne Lang, and the marketing team at BenBella; and The Bromley Group, who consistently make sure the press knows about this book. To Robert Redmond of Nelson Made, for keeping the cyber community informed about this book with www. thebrabook.com and keeping it keyword-savvy and search engine–optimized.

To Joe, Michele, and the team at The Salon in Scarsdale (a.k.a., my own personal "glam squad"), thanks for always keeping me looking presentable, and to Dan Doyle for the fabulous photos.

To Gigi, who was in my belly while I was writing this book but who I cannot thank enough for the extra huge increase in my bra size. I wonder if you'll come out talking about cup sizes and band measurements. To Gizmo and Troubles, for keeping me company all those days and nights I spent locked in the study. To my stepdad Lyle, for making me go to English class, even though it was first period (and for being so much more than a father figure).

Last but not least, to all my parents—Rose and Lyle, Tony and Michele, and Steve and Nina—and the rest of my family, friends, and co-workers, who have been there through thick and thin and utterly supportive the entire time. I could not have achieved this dream without you.

TABLE OF CONTENTS

A Letter from Beverly Johnson

....

Dear Readers of *The Bra Book*:

As I'm writing this, it's been thirty-five years since I first graced the cover of *Vogue* magazine—the first African American model to do so. People say that I am the first black supermodel, which is something I am very proud of. As I look back on my career, I think about what I have gone through as far as body image in an industry that's really all about what you look like on the outside. As a model and actress, as well as a mom, entrepreneur, author, activist, and athlete, I am conscious every day about staying healthy and fit and embracing my body. It's an ongoing process. Like most women, it took me many years to feel comfortable in my own skin.

Growing up in a small town near Buffalo, New York, I was a competitive swimmer, so my body was a vessel for my sport. I wasn't self-conscious about it but I wasn't really conscious of it, either. It was just *there*. Though I was teased by my brother about being "flat as an ironing board," I never internalized it. But I was jealous of my younger sister because she was more "developed" than I was. It seemed the boys were always after her.

1

It wasn't until I became a model and my body was celebrated that I began to think about my breasts. To be honest, it was mostly because I had this dream of becoming a lingerie model. They made double to triple the day rate of us regular models. Those ladies in the Sears catalogs modeling bras and panties made tons of money and I wanted that too! They didn't even need to have big portfolios, just a little bit of cleavage. They were the equivalent of the Victoria's Secret girls of today. In modeling, it was big business. I kept asking my agency to book me for those jobs but I always got the same answer: "You don't have a lingerie body." It finally dawned on me what I was lacking—ample breasts. In the '80s, I had tried this "Thighmaster"-looking thing that you squashed together with your hands to increase your bust size. All the models had this. Every night, I used it fifteen times. Needless to say, it didn't work.

I let go of those dreams and continued to enjoy a successful career in modeling, with more than 500 magazine covers to my credit. For high-fashion and editorial work, they wanted you to look like a "human hanger," which is still the case today, so having boobs was frowned upon. I once overheard a designer say about another model, "Oh, she has these horrible breasts. They are messing up my design; I can't hire her with those big things!" My small stature worked for me.

Whether you are big- or small-busted, this book will educate you not only about bras and your breasts, but how to feel good about what God has given you and how to forever be at peace with your breasts. While many of us curse uncomfortable bras or the appearance of our breasts, what you will read throughout these chapters will teach you how to embrace what you have—and work with it. I wish I'd had a guide like this when I was "growing up" in the fashion industry. No one was there to tell me that what I had was OK, and I always envied others who had what I felt I lacked.

I have learned many lessons over the years, and many have been through trial and error. But one thing I know is that if you feel good about your body, and educate yourself on how to make the most of what you have, you can't go wrong. Whether it's a bra that makes you feel like you have more than you do, or a bra that makes you feel "whole" again after a life-changing mastectomy, it truly can be life-changing when you find the right one. Bras have certainly come a long way since their invention, and in my eyes, so have I. I wish you all the same in your journeys.

Love,
Beverly Johnson

FOREWORD

Ann Deal, **CEO and founder of Fashion Forms**

IN MANY WAYS, A BRA-MAKER HAS TO BE a magician. As founder and CEO of the niche marketer of specialty bras and accessories known worldwide as Fashion Forms, I've learned over the last thirty years in this business that no two women—and no two breasts—are alike. Bra-making is not an exact science, nor can it ever be, given the way our bodies are constructed. The challenge a bra-maker faces is almost the same one a shoe-maker does: everyone's feet are different. Some may be wider; some may be narrower. Often, just like with breasts, women have two feet that are slightly different in size and shape. But all

have to "fit" into one basic sizing system. That's why designing and manufacturing a bra to "fit the masses" truly is a feat of magic. And if the fit isn't right, then the bra isn't going to be successful.

Throughout my extensive career, I have traveled the world over to design and make the best specialty bras and bra accessories. I own and work on patented items for the intimates industry, and sell my patented products and inventions to just about every major retail chain and specialty store in America. I became a dual-citizen of the U.S. and France so I could do business in that country, opened up a distribution center in Canada by invitation from a wonderful chain store there, and do most of my manufacturing in China and the U.S. By utilizing resources around the world, Fashion Forms has become a global brand. And the challenge I am faced with everywhere is the same: how to make a good quality, well-fitting bra that's also innovative enough to meet the needs of consumers who come in completely different shapes and sizes and therefore have different needs.

Every product I've come up with over the years has been due to some sort of demand in the marketplace, but not all of those demands are related to fit. My company brought the original Water Push-up Bra to the U.S. marketplace, where for the first time women were able to expand their bust size with a natural look and feel, without resorting to plastic surgery. I introduced Breast Petals to the world, as well as the breakthrough Backless Strapless Bra.

The bra business really is solutions driven. When halter tops and dresses are in style, so are the bras that can be worn underneath them. If cleavage is all

over the media one year, we bra-makers respond with newer and better push-up bras. In recent times, everyone has been talking about First Lady Michelle Obama's beautifully toned arms. In response, my Strap Connection, which pulls the back of your bra straps together so you can wear shirts that show off your arms, flew off store shelves. Whether you're a Hollywood star preparing for the red carpet, like Raquel Welch, Teri Hatcher, and the other actresses who have come to me for help with those intricate outfits they wear, or just getting dressed for a special occasion, the bra-maker's job is to give you real solutions for your life.

The book you are holding in your hands is another kind of solution. While I and other bra-makers offer solutions, this book will educate you on finding and *utilizing* those solutions. The reason I am in the bra business is to try to help women and to make the industry better, and the need for an educational tool like this book has been present for as long as I can remember. People have always said to me, "You should write a book on bras." Now I'm part of one that I truly believe will be a guide for women everywhere. From helping you find a bra that fits to showing you what's out there that will make your bra work even better, *The Bra Book* will arm you with the right tools and knowledge to find the bra of your dreams.

The motto of Fashion Forms is "imagination is our foundation," and I do imagine a world where women are happy with their bras and walk around with their heads held high feeling good about themselves. My life's work is to help women look and feel shapelier, sexier, and more physically free. One woman wrote that our Breast Petals changed her life. I loved hearing that! I hope that this book and the recommendations in it will change your life as well.

INTRODUCTION

· ·

DURING MY 2004 WEDDING RECEPTION, my best friend Melissa stood up to give a speech that, five years later, is still fresh in my mind. She began with this: "As long as I've known Jené, she has always been searching for the perfect 'one.' The perfect man, the perfect job, the perfect hair color." Naturally, she garnered a laugh from the crowd, but what she said really resonated with me.

As women, we really are always searching for perfection—in bras as in everything else. A woman's quest for the Perfect Bra—the bra that makes her both look good *and* feel good—seems endless.

I've told many women that I've written this book, and not one of them has said she couldn't use a guide like this to help her in her search. In fact, most said, "Why didn't anyone think of this before?!"

In the last thirty-plus years of my life, I've seen bras put women through a range of emotions: denial ("But I'm a size 34C!"), anger ("My bra is SO uncomfortable!"), frustration ("I just can't seem to find one that FITS!"), sadness ("I've now had to switch to a bra that LIFTS!") . . . well, you get the picture. And I always wondered, why wasn't anyone helping us? Why

1

wasn't anyone out there clearing up our confusion about the sizing system, or even just offering basic information about this undergarment that's so essential to our lives?

There are many reasons we all care so much about bras. A good one makes us feel good inside and out. It supports us, even protects us, concealing our flaws and highlighting our strengths. The right one can make us feel confident and sexy—like a woman should!

The bra's ability to change the way we see our breasts, and how that can make us feel, is more important than it sounds. Women in society are often identified—and even judged—by their breasts. Just ask Dolly Parton or Pamela Anderson. And so we tend to judge ourselves by them, too. In my case, my breasts—my "mutant boobs," as I called them—became such a big part of my identity that I didn't even know who *I* was anymore.

I don't remember much about the year I started to notice my body was changing. It was 1986 and my parents were going through a divorce. Growing up an only child in a small town in upstate New York,

I spent a lot of time alone, and there was a McDonald's within walking distance from my house. To compensate for my loneliness, I was eating way too much for my nine-year-old frame. I was awkward, chubby, had bad perms and braces. And I was *different* from the other girls at school.

In middle school it was clear to me that I wasn't developing as fast as the girls around me (although I'm sure I didn't know *how* exactly I was supposed to be developing). I'd look around the locker room after gym class at the other girls and notice they were developing "womanly" features like pubic hair while I was still as bare as a baby's behind. I begged my mom to let me start shaving my legs just like my friends, even though I barely had a hair to snip, just because I desperately wanted to be like everyone else. In choir class, one of my classmates sitting behind me rubbed her finger along my back and shouted, "I don't feel a strap!" While most of the girls in my class were out of training bras by this point, I had never even owned one. So, once again, I begged my mom, and I started wearing one—even though I had nothing to put in it.

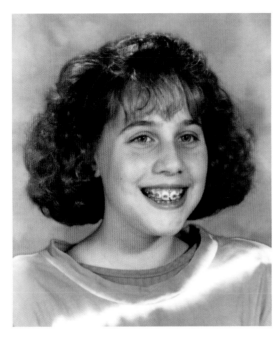

Jené at age 12

year. It was a musical, and I had to kiss a boy! Everyone was impressed by my stellar voice and I was the talk of the school. When high school rolled around, I started cheerleading and won a local modeling contest (I could *not* believe they picked me!). I really started to come out of my shell. But it was also around that time when I realized that there *was* something "wrong" with my body, and it wasn't all in my head. I was still different—not on the inside, but on the *underneath*.

When my breasts had finally developed, I noticed they were unusual. My chest appeared almost concave on one side—my left breast was *much* smaller than the right—and while the right one was round, the left one was more cone-shaped. Our family doctor assured me that nothing was "medically" wrong with me, but that didn't help how I felt when I stood naked in front of the mirror. None of my friends knew; neither did my mom. I wouldn't change in front of other girls in the locker room at school and I even made myself late to class just so I didn't have to. I nearly failed the class directly after gym due to the school's attendance policy, but I

3

The following year I started to grow in leaps and bounds (literally—six inches in one year!) and the baby fat dropped like lightning. The braces came off and the perms, well, they were still there, but I was wearing them well. And although I had my first boyfriend, I still couldn't shake that "fat girl" image I had of myself. I even got the lead in the school play that didn't care. I could never let them see the "real me."

A little piece of fabric and padding known as the Miracle Bra by Victoria's Secret became my saving grace. It had removable pads, which allowed me to remove the padding on the right side but not on the left so that it appeared my breasts were the same shape and size. The company even made swimsuits! But trips with classmates, like our spring break at the beach, were still difficult, because I had to work harder to hide my shameful secret from my girlfriends. And when I hooked up with boys in high school, the bra NEVER came off. I figured if they never knew, then they'd continue to think I was just like any other girl.

After graduating from high school in a class of eighty-something, I entered a college of more than 5,000, and met many more boys. I made the extra effort to hang out with as many of them as possible, just so everyone would know that I was just as attractive as the rest of the girls. It was a sickness, but it fed my self-esteem and my ego. I bonded with a small group of sorority sisters, but I never truly felt like

"one of the girls," always carrying that monkey on my back that made me feel insecure and different from the rest of them—my breasts. Ironically, I spent the summer after my senior year working as a bra-fitter in a Victoria's Secret shop in a local mall, looking at dozens of pairs of breasts each and every day, envying the women who had no problem disrobing in front of me to get measured.

One night, while home completing an internship, I was at the dinner table with my mother and my stepfather. I couldn't hold it in any longer and I broke down in tears. My breasts were taking over my life—they determined my very being and how I looked at myself, and as long as they were "mutant," I would always feel like an alien.

My mother and I went into the bedroom and I finally revealed to her what I'd been hiding so long—the irregular mounds of flesh that had me in their grip and kept me from living my life (and my teenage years) to the fullest. I was nearing graduation by this time and had a job lined up at a local television station. My parents said they would support any decision I made, and despite plastic surgery being relatively unheard of in our small town, they encouraged me to schedule consultations with surgeons. I finished out the year and started my job. I saw more and more clearly that if I were to truly move into the next phase of my life, I had to get this taken care of—no matter the cost (or the pain). I was willing to allow those body parts that identified who I was as a young woman to get slashed and scarred just so I could be "normal." I knew perfection was an unattainable goal. I didn't want perfection; I just wanted my breasts to be like everyone else's.

A few months after graduation I found a surgeon I liked and scheduled the procedure. In it, the surgeon inserted two small saline implants under the muscle (silicone was banned at that time), one larger than the other, to correct the size difference. He then did a breast lift on the right side, attempting to make my right breast the same shape as the left one. The surgery went off without a hitch (minus the expected few days of intense pain and vomiting).

In subsequent years, I relished my newfound freedom. I dated lots of boys and made sure I took off my shirt with each and every one of them. I did everything short of burning my stash of Miracle Bras and bought new ones—without padding. I went braless in halter tops and wore string bikinis. I finally felt normal. I finally felt like I fit in.

But a few years later, after marrying an amazing man named Bill, I entered a statewide pageant for married women. In our dressing room, I looked around at all the other women, many of whom had several kids, and admired their breasts. I noticed once again that my own breasts were different. I hadn't had any kids yet and was barely thirty, but my breasts just didn't look right anymore. It was hard to ignore. My left breast (which was the smaller one originally) once again took on a cone-like shape and became distorted, so it looked as if I had one breast on top of the other. My right breast sagged terribly.

The scars from my first surgery had healed well, but I soon began to realize that those wounds might have to be re-opened. Of course this meant not just physical wounds, but emotional ones as well. My

5

husband said he didn't care what my breasts looked like—that he loved me for who I was—but then I started getting the pains. They were dull but stabbing, and occurred near the bottom of my left breast. I dreaded the thought of surgery again. And as wonderful as the Miracle Bra was, this wasn't something it alone was going to be able to fix. I couldn't help thinking, *When will my breasts finally stop ruling my life?*

The first doctor I saw gave me the answer I had been desperately wanting for so long—she diagnosed me with Tubular Breast Syndrome, a condition or defect that causes one or both breasts to develop with a tube-like shape. I had a bona-fide syndrome—something I was probably born with and something I couldn't have prevented! The doctor said I was also suffering a common complication from the implant in my left breast, which was what had likely caused the pain, as well as the breast hardening and distortion. The doctor said I was right to come in and that I should get the problem taken care of, although I had a high risk of having the same complication happen again with a new set of implants.

My mother asked if I had considered just having the implants taken out, but I simply couldn't. Maybe it was vanity, maybe it wasn't, but I could never, ever go back to the way I used to feel. I had grown up a lot since then—I was more complete on the inside and I knew I'd always be beautiful no matter what—but I could never forget the way I felt all those years.

I went ahead with the surgery to replace the old implants, and as I write this, it has been just five days since I woke up with a new set of implants, silicone this time. My "girls," as I now affectionately call them, look wonderful. I feel ready to move on now, and even though I know I will likely have to get the implants replaced in ten years, I feel whole again.

Why am I telling you all this in a book about bras? My breasts have been a part of my identity for a long time. They've been the source of so much of my anxiety, and that's a hard habit to break. But I'm willing to try—and sharing my story with others is part of that. There is not a woman on this earth who can't identify with body image issues—and many of those issues revolve around our breasts. As women, we are much harder on ourselves than we should be. How our breasts look and feel has the power, for good or for ill, to change how we look and feel. And bras are a big part of that. Wearing the right bra can provide a much-needed "boost," both in confidence and otherwise. As in my case for all those years, they can even make you simply feel "normal." It's a powerful little piece of fabric!

My goal with this book is to educate and, I hope, empower you. While the bra is now a centenarian, its hundred-year presence in our wardrobes doesn't change the fact that many of us still feel we are venturing into unknown territory. Oprah helped make us aware, when she declared that America needed a Bra Intervention. On her talk show, Tyra Banks actually held a *bra burning*, showing exactly how frustrated, sad, and

angered we are by our bras. The reason? We don't understand them—and until now there hasn't been a place where all the information we need was accurately and succinctly pulled together so that we finally could. *The Bra Book* takes away the mystery by showing you not only how your bra works, but how to make it work for *you*.

Whether you have embraced your breasts your entire life or been adversely affected by them in some way, as I have, this book will give you the support you need—in more ways than one. Just like your best girlfriend or your mom, this book will, I hope, be a comforting voice on your journey to feeling confident in your skin *and* your bra. The only emotion your bra should evoke is happiness—and after *The Bra Book*, it will be. Do you need any more reason to turn the page than that?

7

one

The Herstory
of
Bras

EVERY WOMAN HAS A "HERSTORY." SOME OF IT SHE'D LIKE TO REMEMBER, and some of it she'd rather forget. But when it comes to a woman's herstory with bras, there are often many memorable moments.

No matter how old we get, we often still remember our major bra milestones. Remember when Mom took you to the local department store to buy your very first training bra (even though you most likely had nothing to go in it)? Or how about when you realized that a little padding goes a long way?

"The bra is with us through every stage of life," says Mara Susskind Kalcheim, an intimate apparel industry expert who has been in the business for more than forty years. "As a young girl, you are dying for your first bra. As a young woman, you want a sexy bra to wear for your first boyfriend and something that will support developing breasts. As you grow into motherhood, you need a maternity bra and bras that will fit your changing figure. In your thirties and forties, [you need] something more steady and supportive but still sexy, and then as you get older, you go for comfort!"

While it's no doubt the bra has left a large imprint on our personal pasts, that little piece of fabric with the molded cups and many pseudonyms ("over-the-shoulder boulder holder," "brassiere," "corset") has left many a mark on our society as well! Like reporter Samantha Thompson Smith says in her 2007 article for McClatchy Newspapers: "Love it, hate it, burn it, or embrace it, the bra endures!" Over the years the bra has even become a fashion icon in its own right.

Before you can learn about all the bra has to offer, it's important to understand how the bra came to be. Here is a mostly factual, if somewhat tongue-in-cheek, roundup of some of the highlights of the century-long herstory of the bra.

The Herstory of Bras

▶ **1907**: French couturier Paul Poiret loosens up the corset (a binding garment used for centuries to cinch the waist and support the breasts) and makes the first "brassiere." *Vogue* magazine coins the term.

12

▼ **1913**: The bra as we know it is born when socialite Mary Phelps Jacob fashions together two hankies with some pink ribbon and cord. Friends encourage her to patent her design and a year later she sells it to Warner Brothers Corset Company.[1]

1917: The U.S. enters World War I and women are asked to stop wearing corsets to conserve steel. Some 28,000 tons

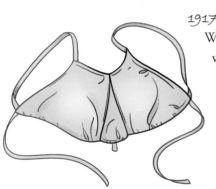

[1]While Jacob is perhaps the most well-known bra creator in history, many others would claim they actually "invented" the bra, including Maidenform founder Ida Rosenthal.

are diverted, enough to build an entire battleship.

▶ 1920s: Binding "flapper bras" are all the rage. Flat chests are in and big busts are taboo.

▶ (far right) 1930s: Advertisements aren't allowed to show photographs of women in bras so savvy companies use drawings of models instead!

1935: Cleavage starts to make a comeback. Founders of Maidenform Co. introduce "cup sizes" from A to D.[2]

For the first time, "getting an A" is considered a bad thing.

1939: The word "bra" is officially added to the English dictionary

13

Bra Herstory Fact

Rome wasn't built in a day and neither was the bra. Did you know some say the bra dates all the way back to 2000 B.C.? This early corset-style bra was open at the front to the waist, leaving the breasts uncovered. Small strips of leather curved around the outline of the breasts for support.

[2]Although there are conflicting reports on the date Maidenform actually began selling these different cup sizes, some say it was as early as 1922!

14

▼ (bottom) 1947: Kleenex sales plummet when Frederick's of Hollywood unveils the world's first padded bra and, a year later, the push-up bra. Boys everywhere rejoice.

◀ 1950s: Missile or "bullet-shaped" bras that create a pointed appearance under sweaters gain prevalence. Hollywood's A-list actresses, including Jayne Mansfield, capitalize on the trend.

1951: Wrapture's blow-up bra leaves wearers breathless when they have to inflate their own cups using an attached straw. "We must, we must, we must increase our bust" becomes the mantra for a generation, and women everywhere begin exercising their chest muscles in hopes of increasing their, er, size.

(although "brassiere" has been in the Oxford dictionary since 1912). Little did we know "bootylicious" would follow suit just a few decades later.

▲ 1941: World War II brings a shortage of the metals and other materials used to make bras and corsets, so synthetic fibers like nylon are used as an alternative.

1958: DuPont introduces Lycra, a fiber that can stretch significantly while still retaining its shape, allowing

bras, although none are ever confirmed to have actually been on fire.

1969: A woman in San Francisco publicly removes her bra during "Anti-Bra Day," a day to protest the pressures society puts on women.

That same year, the medical community warns women of the adverse effects of going braless.

1977: Athletic gals finally get some support, too, when the Jogbra is introduced. The world's first "sports bra" consists of two male jockstraps, sewn together (yikes!).

1983: The Material Girl shows the world less "material" is more. Madonna shocks fans (but cements her place in fashion history) by wearing her bra as a top while promoting her debut

15

corsets and bras to be more lightweight, comfortable, and breathable. Gals everywhere breathe a sigh of bra-lief!

▲ **1968:** The bra—or lack thereof—becomes an icon of American history and a symbol of feminism when protestors hurl their bras into trashcans during the Miss America pageant in Atlantic City. Media reports claim the pro-women's liberation crowd is burning the

Bra Herstory Fact

A *Time* magazine article dating to 1965 cites the average price of bras at just $4.

album. It won't be the only time Madonna makes news in a bra.

1985: Perhaps a nod to the growing popularity of breast augmentation, manufacturers like Frederick's of Hollywood start offering sizes above a DD.

▼ 1986: Frederick's of Hollywood opens the country's first "Bra Museum," housing lingerie worn by celebrities from the previous four decades. The museum garners national attention just six years later when it is looted during the Los Angeles riots. Looters reportedly snatch a pair of Ava Gardner's "bloomers," among other items.

16

A corset designed by Diana Ross currently housed in Frederick's of Hollywood's flagship store, the site of the former museum.

1989: Not leaving smaller-busted women behind, Frederick's unveils the first silicone breast enhancers (they get placed inside the bra), which come to be known as "chicken cutlets." They become the first "food" ever embraced by Hollywood starlets.

◀ 1990: The bra hits a high "point" when Madonna's highly controversial cone-shaped style stuns folks in cities all across America during her Blonde Ambition World Tour. People everywhere are warned, "Kids, don't try these at home. They'll put your eye out!"

That same year, a Japanese company develops the world's largest bra. It has an under-bust measurement of 78'8", and a bust measurement of 91'10", according to *The Guinness Book of World Records*

> ### Bra Herstory Fact
>
> Although breasts come in all shapes and sizes, the "ideal" shape of a woman's bosoms under her blouse is dictated by what's popular in society at the time. In the 1920s women flattened their breasts, and just a few decades later wore bras to make them look pointier. In the twenty-first century, women have been going under the knife to attain the roundest breasts possible.

◀ 1994: "Hello, boys." The Wonderbra, a plunging push-up bra, goes on sale in the U.S. and chaos ensues. The company claims one is sold every fifteen seconds.

1995: Men get their first bra, if only on television. On an episode of the hit show *Seinfeld*, Kramer and Frank Costanza hatch a plan to sell a Velcro-fastened bra for men, but can't decide whether to call it the "bro" or the "mansiere."

▼ 1997: Fashion Forms introduces the Original Water Bra, a bra filled with water and oil (to keep the water from evaporating) that revolutionizes the push-up bra industry. It makes headlines when David Letterman tries to run over one with a truck and Jennifer Aniston reportedly has hers attacked by a chopstick.

1998: Tara Cavosie of Albany, New York, creates the first "backless strapless bra." Fashion Forms makes the bra and retailers like Victoria's Secret and Neiman Marcus quickly scoop it up. Clearly filling a consumer need, it flies off store shelves.

Back by Popular Demand
The One And Only
"THE ORIGINAL"
Water Push-Up Bra

> **Bra Herstory Fact**
>
> Us gals are growing. Published reports say that, in the last twenty years, the most popular bra size has increased from a 34B to a 36C!

1999: The Water Bra gets another fifteen minutes of fame on an episode of the sitcom *Will and Grace*. Debra Messing's character, Grace, wears the bra, only to have it "spring a leak" during an evening out. The Water Bra has since gone the way of the waterbed as a fad that has seemed to fizzle out, although it is still available for purchase online.

2004: Singer Janet Jackson sends censors into a flurry when, braless, she reveals a nipple during a Super Bowl performance on national television. The incident is attributed to a "wardrobe malfunction."

That same year, actress Tara Reid accidentally exposes her breast on the red carpet, further cementing the importance of wearing a bra (even under a slinky evening gown).

2005: Supermodel Karolina Kurkova sets tongues wagging in a $13 million diamond bra on the Victoria's Secret runway.

▼ **2006**: The daytime talk show queens get everyone talking about bras! *The Oprah Winfrey Show* holds a "Bra Intervention." Oprah, known for covering "of the moment" topics and hot-button issues, declares: "America, you are wearing the wrong bra," and counts herself among the 85 percent of women believed to be incorrectly underclothed. A media blitz on the topic ensues. Supermodel turned talk-show diva Tyra Banks follows suit, devoting an episode of *The Tyra Banks Show* to throwing an on-set "panty party" and teaching viewers how to find properly fitting undergarments.

Due to what comes to be known as the "Oprah Winfrey Effect," bra sales go up

15 percent the following year, to $5.7 billion, according to the NPD Group, a research firm in Port Washington, New York.

▲ 2007: The bra turns 100 and continues to change with the times. In line with growing concern over the global warming crisis, the bra goes green when manufacturers start making bras using eco-friendly fabrics like bamboo blends.

2008: *The Tyra Banks Show* holds a ceremonial "bra burning," with Tyra encouraging audience members and viewers to get rid of ill-fitting undergarments.

That same year, the bra gets "ink" in major magazines like *InStyle*, *US Weekly*, *Cosmopolitan*, and *Real Simple* with features such as "Celeb Bra Blunder" roundups, tips for finding your "best bra," and the proper ways to care for your bra. Blogs, too, are abuzz with all things bras, especially celebrity "support slipups" by Britney Spears, Drew Barrymore, and others.

▼ 2009: Women's perceptions of bra sizes are changing! An article cites DD as "the new C" as more and more women get fitted and learn their true sizes. Retailers respond with offerings like larger cup sizes and more size combinations.

That same year, *The Bra Book* is published. Women everywhere finally have a guide to the world's most confusing undergarment!

19

Remember when you learned your ABCs? Continue on to Chapter 2, where you'll learn them all over again—the ABCs of bras!

two

The ABCs

of

Bras

CHANCES ARE, IF YOU'RE OLD ENOUGH TO READ THIS BOOK, THEN YOU know by now that the letters of the alphabet also correlate to the cup sizes of bras. Cup sizes range from AA to JJ and are anything but consistent—in fact, despite there *theoretically* being a standard for sizing, it can vary from vendor to vendor.

But there's a lot more to the "ABCs" of bras than just figuring out the cup sizing system. With more than forty separate components, a bra has enough engineering to make NASA envious! In fact, in an interview on NBC's *Today* show, Maidenform executive Manette Scheininger compared the bra to a suspension bridge, saying, "a bra and a bridge have to support and they have to be flexible. So a bra has to support the weight of the breast but it has to be flexible enough to move with the body because you want to be comfortable. And a bridge has to be supportive for the cars moving across it, but again, it has to be flexible for wind conditions and just the movement of the cars."

Luckily you don't need a degree in physics to get the basics of how your bra works. Understanding your bra can be as simple as A-B-C.

ANATOMY, BIOMECHANICS, AND PHYSICS: THE SCIENCE OF BRAS

. . . .

While our bras do many things for us—shape our breasts, create a smooth line under clothing, and boost our confidence—the garment's most important job is providing support.

So how exactly do bras do this? According to Christi Anderson, co-founder of Zyrra (a company that hosts in-home bra fitting parties and specializes in custom bras), it really comes down to basic physics. Think of the breast "as a weight that we're trying to lift up. Gravity pulls it down, but something needs to counteract the pull." Breast tissue is supported naturally by our chest muscles, skin, and ligaments—but

they alone aren't enough to fight off the effects of gravity. Our bras do what our bodies alone cannot.

Some researchers say bras have only recently become a "science." A 2007 study at the University of Portsmouth in England looked at bra design and what it's doing for our bodies. In an article on the website LiveScience, the study's author Joanna Scurr is quoted as saying that, previously in bra design, "there was no research. It's like designing a car or kitchen equipment without first thinking 'what is the purpose of this?'"

The lack of research could be in part because the anatomy of our breasts is something of a puzzle. A woman's breasts can range from 10 ounces all the way up to 20 pounds or more in weight, and there is no definitive rhyme or reason to their structure. They are mostly made up of lobes and a network of ducts designed to produce milk. The rest of the breast is fat, tissue, and skin. Why exactly our breasts sag is a mystery, too. While many anatomists believe the connective breast tissue known as Cooper's ligaments provides our breasts' main support, others feel the skin plays the most important role in holding our breasts in place. Unfortunately, there are no definitive answers.

Scientists are also still trying to figure out exactly how our breasts move, and how a bra can best counteract that motion. In 2007, a group of biomechanists in Australia did a study on breast movement where they fitted seventy subjects with specially designed bras. According to a 2005 article in *Discover* magazine, they placed sensors under the straps to measure how much pressure was placed on the shoulders. They also placed electrodes on the subjects' torsos and necks to monitor muscle activity and LEDs on their sternums and nipples, and on the bra's straps, to measure breast

and torso movements. While the women all walked, jogged, and ran, the scientists were able to track their breasts' pattern of movement (it resembled a figure eight), how much their breasts moved, and how that movement was affected by wearing the bra. Obviously, larger breasts moved much more than the smaller breasts—although tests found that even A-cups move up to an average of 40mm (that's just under two inches, or about the length of a large paperclip) from their natural resting place. A 2007 British study found that breasts move in three directions during exercise: up and down, side to side, and forward and back. And while no one really knows for sure the long-term implications of such breast movements, it's presumed that they can cause breast pain and are the most likely reason for sagging.

What all these studies have confirmed is that the larger the breasts, the more they move. And the more breasts move, the more momentum they have. A well-designed bra stops that momentum. How? Let's take a look at the working parts of the bra, and the way they work together to give you the best possible support.

25

The Parts *of the* Bra

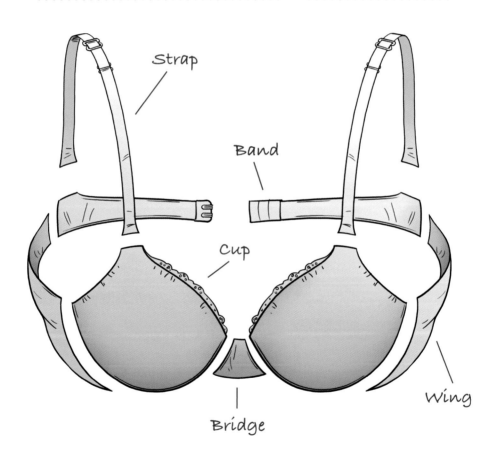

Strap

Band

Cup

Bridge

Wing

Simply Strapping: The straps are the parts of the bra that loop over your shoulders. Bra straps offer support but not primarily by holding the breasts up. Instead, they support the breasts by stabilizing them. They are also one of the few adjustable parts of the bra.

In that 2005 breast movement study, scientists found that the straps bear the brunt of the load generated by momentum during physical activity. And while the straps are obviously important for support, they shouldn't bear the *entire* burden. According to Zyrra co-founder Anderson, in a well-designed bra the straps only *help* with the lifting. You'll know they are being overworked if they are digging into your shoulders and causing you discomfort.

To get the most support out of your bra straps, keep them on the tightest setting possible that does not cause you pain or discomfort. *Tip:* Start by making the straps as tight as possible and then loosen them up from there.

I'm with the Band: The band is the part of the bra that wraps around the ribcage just below the breasts. The band is the

> ### The ABCs of Bras Fast Fact
>
> Hate having to readjust your bra straps every time you wear or wash your bra? It could be worse—your grandmother just had to put up with straps that were too loose. Adjusting your bra straps wasn't even an option until the 1940s!

27

most important element of support because it holds the bra's cups (and the breast tissue within them) in place.

You can look at the bra like a teeter-totter—the more the band rides up in the back, the more the cups will come down in the front. Because of this, the band should fit snugly (but not too snugly; you should be able to fit one or two fingers underneath it) and lie completely level across your back. If it's too loose, it will ride up your back, allowing your breasts to sag.

She's Got Wings: The wings are the parts of the bra band that stretch from the side of the cup around the back to the place the band fastens. The wings provide most of the cup support by counterbalancing the weight of the breasts in front.

Captivating Cups: The cups are the parts of the bra that hold the breast tissue in place and act as the breasts' main means of support. They can also help to push breasts up and inward, creating cleavage.

Properly fitted cups should provide enough support to prevent the straps from digging into your shoulders. A cup with underwire is the most supportive—it allows the breasts' weight to be more evenly distributed to the straps and around the band.

Bridging the Gap: The bridge is the small piece of fabric located between the bra's cups. It may be a tiny piece of your overall bra, but it is actually an important part of proper support because it holds the cups at the front of the body, preventing the breasts from moving too far to either side. The bridge should fit completely flush against the body. "Without a bridge that sits flat," Anderson says, "the breasts would be pulled off to the sides by the force of the band."

Look at your bra like a puzzle—it's only complete (and properly supportive!) when all the "pieces" are put together properly. If they aren't, then your bra will not be doing its job—which could lead to discomfort in the present, and sagging in the future.

Getting to Know Your Bra

from A *to* Z

There's more to understanding bras than just knowing their working parts. Bras today come in all kinds of styles and all kinds of fabrics. Now that you know how the bra works, you need to understand the jargon that describes all the different bras available to you (and other important terms related to the bra).

The next few pages teach you all this information the old-fashioned way: with a bra alphabet!

Adhesive or Backless Strapless Bra: A bra that lacks straps and a back band and is held up by medical-grade adhesive.

Balconette (or Balconet) Bra: A bra that covers only the lower part of the breasts. The cups are usually cut in a straight line across each breast.

Bandeau Bra: A band of fabric that covers the breasts. It's usually stretchy and without straps, but sometimes has built-in cups.

Bra: When you look up bra in the dictionary, you are referred to the definition for brassiere, which according to Merriam-Webster is a noun for "a woman's undergarment to cover and support the breasts."

Bralette: A soft bra that has no underwire or structured cups. It resembles a camisole but instead of covering the midsection stops just short of the tummy with an elastic band.

Breast Petal: A small adhesive nipple cover that prevents the nipple from protruding under sheer garments.

Bustier: A bra that extends down over the midsection and usually has boning (small vertical support tubes made of metal or plastic) designed to push up the breasts. It's often worn under a wedding gown and resembles a corset.

Cleavage: The effect attained by pushing the breasts together to create a vertical line down the middle.

30

Compression Bra: A sports bra that presses (or *compresses*) breast tissue against the body to restrict its movement during exercise or other activity.

Contour Bra: A bra with lined or padded cups that hold their shape even when not being worn. According to lingerie reference intimateguide.com, the bra "offers significant coverage, a smooth shape, and hides the nipples—even under tight clothing."

Convertible Bra: A bra that can be worn multiple ways through the use of detachable straps. For example, you can wear it with a strap over each shoulder like a normal bra, but you can also take one strap off and wrap the other around your neck and hook it in the front to turn it into a halter bra. The convertible bra is versatile and can be adjusted to remain invisible under almost any neckline.

Corset-Style Bra: A bra designed to have the same aesthetic as the corset, a garment that was once worn

to mold the torso into a desired shape, but without the painful waist-whittling. They also push up the bust, much like a bustier.

Cotton: A natural fiber that is used to make many bras, especially those intended primarily for comfort. Cotton textiles are soft, cozy, fine, and breathable. They absorb moisture and are easy to wear and care for. According to atlastbras.com, the online home of Sacramento, California, store At Last . . . Bras and Lingerie, "Different qualities in cotton are dictated by how long and how fine the fiber is spun. The longer and finer the fiber is, the more valuable cotton becomes" (and the better the quality of the bra).

Cutlet: A gel pad that is made to be inserted inside a bra, under the breast tissue, to create a fuller look or boost up the breast. It is called a cutlet because of its not-so-subtle resemblance to actual chicken cutlets.

Cookie: No, not the kind you eat. This is the oval-shaped removable fabric pad usually

31

found in push-up bras. It does basically the same thing as a cutlet, but isn't as "natural" in look or feel.

Front-Close Bra: A bra that has a plastic barrel closure or zipper in the front instead of the typical hook-and-eye closure in the back.

Demi (or Demi-Cup) Bra: A bra that covers the lower three-quarters of the breast and is great for pushing up breast tissue and creating cleavage.

Full-Coverage Bra: A bra with cups that extend well above the nipple. This is the best bra style for larger breasts because it provides more coverage and support.

Double-Sided Tape: An adhesive tape that is coated with adhesive on both sides. It is designed to stick two lightweight surfaces together and can be used to hold a bra in place beneath a dress or top.

Graduated Padding: A bra-padding technique in which more padding is used near the bottom of the cup and then gradually lightened toward the top, providing a more natural looking push-up. In traditional padded bras, the cup is padded evenly all over.

Encapsulation Bra: A sports bra that has a separate cup for each breast (unlike the compression sports bra, where the breasts are treated as one mass).

Hidden Underwire Bra: A bra that has no seam separating the cups from the underwire, concealing the underwire from view and often offering greater comfort to the wearer.

32

Inner Sling: A soft strip of fabric inside a bra that follows the bottom curve of the cup, similar to an underwire, to provide added support.

Kleenex: A type of padding once used by teenage girls to "stuff their bras." With all the padding options out there today (see *Cookie*, *Cutlet*, and *Push-Up Bra*), Kleenex is rarely needed anymore—at least for this purpose!

Lace: An ornamental fabric made of net-like threads sewn by hand or machine. It is often used in bras and other lingerie to create a sexy appearance.

Lycra: A stretch fiber, or spandex, that is a registered trademark of Invista, formerly DuPont. It is the most recognized and popular brand of spandex throughout the world, and many designers and clothing manufacturers use it in their products. Lycra is used in fabric blends alongside cotton, silk, and synthetic fibers, and is popular in bras and swimwear. It allows garments to be more lightweight, comfortable, and breathable. It is also quick-drying and resistant to bacteria, ultraviolet (UV) rays, and chlorine.

Mastectomy Bra: A bra that is specially designed for women who have had one or more breasts removed in surgery, called a mastectomy. It has special pockets to hold a prosthesis breast, or "mastectomy form," in place.

Maternity Bra: A bra that is specially designed for women who are pregnant. It offers wider straps to increase support and reduce bounce, as well as more comfortable material to prevent breast tissue irritation, since pregnant women often have swelling and tenderness in the breasts.

Microfiber: A fabric often used in bras, especially t-shirt bras. According to atlastbras.com,

33

microfiber is "made from polyester and polyamide that's finer than the finest silk thread. [Its threads] are particularly soft, pliable and pleasant on the skin, offering maximum comfort."

Minimizer: A bra designed for larger-breasted women who wish to create the illusion of smaller breasts. According to intimateguide.com, this bra "reduces the projection of the wearer's breasts by holding the breast tissue snugly and redistributing breast flesh more toward the underarm and the center front."

Molded Cup: A bra cup that is created by a heat and pressure process that molds fabric into shape. Also known as seamless cups (because the process results in no visible fabric seams), molded cups are often found in contour bras and in t-shirt bras, and are nearly invisible under clothes.

Nursing Bra: A bra that is specially designed for women who are nursing. Like a maternity bra, it offers extra support, but it also has cup

34

openings to allow for breastfeeding without removing the entire bra.

Oprah Winfrey: Television's talk show queen, credited with putting bras back in the spotlight when she declared America needed a "Bra Intervention" in 2005.

Pastie: A decorative covering that is meant to conceal just the nipple while leaving the rest of the breast bare. It is usually applied with a special glue or tape.

Plunge Bra: A bra with a center that dips low between the breasts in front so that only cleavage is revealed under low-cut garments.

Fashion Forms makes a "U"-cut version with a lower-than-normal band that allows the center to dip several inches below the middle of the breasts.

Push-Up Bra: A bra with padded cups that is designed to press the breasts upward and create a fuller appearance.

Q is the quest for the perfect bra. You are one step closer, simply by reading this book!

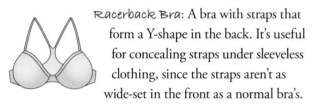

Racerback Bra: A bra with straps that form a Y-shape in the back. It's useful for concealing straps under sleeveless clothing, since the straps aren't as wide-set in the front as a normal bra's.

Rayon: A synthetic silk-like fabric that is used in bras and many articles of clothing because of its low cost and high versatility.

Satin: A smooth fabric of silk or rayon that is often used in bras. It has a glossy face and a dull back.

Silicone: A clear compound used in gel pads that are placed into bra cups to increase bust size, in some breast implants, and on the inside of the band on strapless bras to prevent slippage by "gripping" the skin. It is composed of both organic and inorganic polymers, and is created through a specific chemical formula.

Strapless Bra: An underwire bra with no straps that is often worn with special occasion attire or other complicated tops where bra straps would be visible. This bra *sounds* simple (i.e., a bra without straps), but it can be difficult

35

to find one that fits properly and doesn't slide down the body when worn.

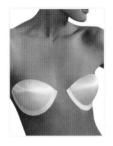

Support Adhesive: A lightweight foam bra "cup" that is coated with adhesive so it can stick to the skin, providing bra-like support without the bulk of a full bra.

Viscose: A soft rayon fabric that is very similar to cotton or silk. It is made from purified cellulose, which usually comes from specially processed wood pulp.

36

T-Shirt Bra: A bra with molded cups that is often smooth and seamless so it appears "invisible" under t-shirts or other thin tops.

X-Back Bra: A bra with straps that crisscross in the back to form an X-shape. Much like the racerback or Y-back bra, it allows the wearer to avoid showing her straps in tops that have narrow shoulders and backs (and prevents her straps from slipping off her shoulders).

Underwire: A piece of metal that is sewn into the bra under the cup to lift and shape the bust. It is used as an additional means of supporting the breasts.

Zip-Front Bra: A bra that closes with a zipper in the front. Zip-fronts usually only appear on sports bras.

Now that you've learned the basics, you're ready to move on to the most important aspect of the bra: fit! Read on for the dos and don'ts of bra fit, and how to make sure you're wearing the right size.

three

Like a Glove

Finding the perfect fit

As we know, not all busts are created equal. That's why, when it comes to bras, there are several different cup sizes and band measurements for a woman to choose from, to ensure her bra is a perfect fit. But what really constitutes a "perfect" fit, and does such perfection exist? Most experts will tell you that it's tough to attain "perfection" when it comes to bras, short of spending hundreds of dollars to have one custom-made for your body. But what you can do is follow some simple rules to at least find one that fits you well.

Chances are the bra you are wearing now *doesn't*. Statistics show (and Oprah said it, too) that 85 percent of us are wearing the wrong bra size altogether! But how could that be? "I have been a 34C for years!" you say. This common denial could be costing you the comfort and support you deserve. I was smug when I met with Frederika Zappe, the nationally renowned bra fit expert for Eveden, convinced she wasn't going to tell *me* anything new. But boy was I ever wrong! Wrong cup size, wrong band measurement—you guessed it—wrong bra! Once she put me in the right size, I immediately looked thinner and more proportioned, and even my posture improved. A co-worker the next day even asked me if I had lost weight!

The information and tips in this chapter will help you understand how your bra is supposed to fit and why it's so important to get it right. And in the end, even if you haven't yet achieved "perfection," at least you'll be standing a little taller.

WHY DO WE
GET IT WRONG?

. . . .

Finding the right bra is like finding a good man. Many women I know are consistently choosing Mr. Wrong. And after years in a bad relationship, they go right out and find another man who doesn't call when he says he will, shows clear disregard for their feelings, and ultimately breaks their hearts. While our bras aren't likely to break our hearts, they can let us down, failing us when we need them the most. And although they won't forget our anniversary, they certainly won't last us till the next one (it's recommended we replace our bras every six months to a year).

I can't explain why women continue to choose the wrong men (I'll leave that one to Dr. Laura), but I can offer up two main explanations as to why we consistently choose the wrong bra.

The first has to do with size. Figuring out your correct size is tough, and most of us don't know what a properly sized bra really looks like.

The second has to do with quality. Bras may be skimpy, but they're nothing to skimp on. Don't let your pocketbook affect your judgment. Most women don't realize that investing just a little bit more in the right bra can make all the difference in their daily lives. "You get what you pay for in bras," says Tara Cavosie, a bra designer for Fashion Forms. "Spend a little more money and get one that's well-made and fits great. It's going to look better and fit better for the whole year. It's simply going to last you longer. And we're not talking hundreds of dollars, just a little bit more of an investment."

The second is up to you, but I can give you some tips on the first!

41

"America, you are wearing the wrong bra!"
– Oprah Winfrey

How You Can Tell You Are

If 85 percent of us are wearing the wrong one, chances are most of us don't even know it. The first rule of thumb? If your bra causes you pain in any way, it doesn't fit properly.

Here are some other basic warning signs that you are wearing an ill-fitting bra (plus solutions for each):

FROM THE BACK

The Problem: The shoulder straps fall down or dig in.
The Solution: The straps may simply need to be adjusted. Or in the case of dig-in, you may need a larger band or cup size.

The Problem: The band either rides up or slides down in the back, instead of remaining somewhat "level" all the way around your body, or squeezes your flesh in a way that causes pain or leaves marks.
The Solution: You likely need a different band size. If the bra band slides downward, you need a smaller size; if it rides up or causes bulging, you need to go larger.

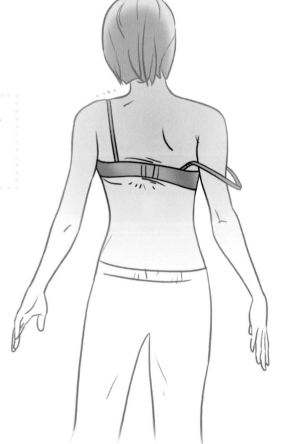

Wearing the Wrong One

FROM THE FRONT

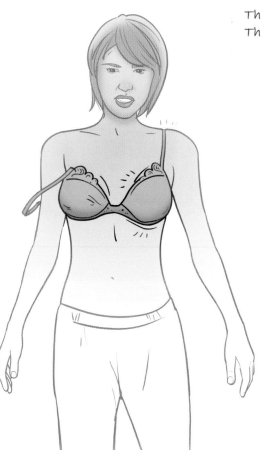

The Problem: The cups are baggy, gaping, or wrinkly.
The Solution: You need a smaller cup size.

The Problem: The underwire isn't flush against your ribcage or is cutting into the underside of your breasts.
The Solution: You need a larger cup size.

The Problem: Your nipples pop out of the cups, or your breast tissue billows out of the top, creating a "double boob" effect.
The Solution: You need either a larger cup size or a fuller-coverage bra.

The Problem: The bridge of the bra doesn't lie flat against your body.
The Solution: You need a larger band or cup size.

43

How to Find the Right One

Your first step in finding the right bra is getting "sized up." Visit a bra or lingerie store that has bra fitters on hand, and let them work their magic (leave your modesty at home). Many women have never been fitted at all, while others haven't been fitted in a long time. It's important to remember that due to changes in our bodies (which will be discussed in detail in Chapters 5 and 6), you need to get re-fitted every six months to a year!

Most malls contain a Victoria's Secret, which specially trains employees on how to fit bras in its very own "bra room." Department stores like Neiman Marcus

"I didn't even know my bra size until I made a movie."

– Angelina Jolie

and Bloomingdale's also often have lingerie departments (JCPenney recently expanded theirs!) with employees who are equipped to take your measurements (in the case of Bloomingdale's, they are actually "certified"). And it's free! Another option is to visit a local seamstress and have her measure you. But for starters, you can get a rough approximation of your size by measuring yourself.

The most important thing is to get educated *before* you walk into the store, so that the salesperson is merely there to assist you, as opposed to relying on the store's salesperson completely (in some cases, you will know more than they do). The end result will be the best possible bra for you!

HOW BRA SIZES WORK

Your bra size contains two important parts:

▶ An even number that represents the circumference of your ribcage below your breasts and describes your band size

▶ A letter that describes your cup size

While this sounds simple, it isn't. There are many misconceptions about what these numbers mean.

> ### Like a Glove Fit Tip
> What about strapless? A great-fitting strapless bra can be tricky to find. But it's easy to tell when it's wrong—it's either sliding down your body and off your breasts completely, or it's cutting your breasts horizontally, giving you the dreaded "four-boobs."

45

For starters, band size doesn't necessarily equal the number of inches your ribcage measures around. Your band size is estimated *based* on the width of your ribcage, but it isn't an exact science. You often have to add one or two inches—or even up to four or *five*—to get your correct band size, depending on manufacturer and style. A 34 in one bra may feel just right while a 34 in another may be too tight. (I'll explain in greater detail in "Your Bra Size," below.)

Like a Glove Fit Tip

You've heard of Tupperware parties and Mary Kay gatherings, but bra fit fiestas? There are companies that do just that! One such company, The Uplifting Makeover (www. bramakeover.com), will host a "fit" party for you and all of your girlfriends in the comfort of your own home. You can then choose from a selection of bras from various brands.

Figuring out your cup size isn't easy either. It's calculated *in relation to* your band size. The size of an A-cup—the volume an A-cup holds—changes depending on the band size. An A-cup on a 32 band is not the same as an A-cup on a 34 band, and so on.

Let's say you are in your favorite lingerie store and you spot a bra you

absolutely *have* to have. However, you are a 34C and they don't have your size. What to do? Because of the way bra sizing works, you may be able to go up a band size and down a cup size and still achieve a similar fit—you might be able to go with the 36B instead. Just because a B is thought to be smaller than a C doesn't mean it actually is. A B is just smaller than a C in the same band size. Why? The snugger band size decreases the width and depth of the cup, which means the 34C, while smaller than the 36C, actually holds the same *volume* of breast tissue as the 36B. This trick can be particularly useful for larger cup sizes. For example, I am currently wearing a 34G, which can be a tough size to find. When I found a bra style I really liked and it didn't come in a G cup, I opted to try the 36F instead. It worked perfectly!

The best way to really understand this is to go into a store and compare bra cups on different size bands. If you compare a 38A to a 34A, the 38A's cup will be obviously bigger. But if you compare a 38A and 34D, the cups will be much closer in size. This doesn't mean that these two sizes are interchangeable, however; you

BUYING BRAS OVERSEAS

While sizes vary by manufacturer, they also vary by country. With the internet making international shopping easy, and more U.S. stores importing international brands, you may find that you want to buy a European- or Australian-made bra. Check the charts below for your international size conversion.

BRAS – BAND SIZES

USA	UK	Euro	French	Italian	Australian
28	28				
30	30				
32	32	70	85	1	10
34	34	75	90	2	12
36	36	80	95	3	14
38	38	85	100	4	16
40	40	90	105	5	18
42	42				
44	44				
46	46				
48	48				
50	50				
52	52				
54	54				
56	56				

BRAS – CUP SIZES

USA	UK	Euro	French	Italian	Australian
AA	AA	AA	AA		
A	A	A	A	A	A
B	B	B	B	B or None	B
C	C	C	C	C	C
D	D	D	D	D	D
DD/E	DD	E	E	DD	DD
DDD/F	E	F	F	E	E
G	FF			F	F
H	FF				FF
I	G				G
J	GG				GG
K	H				HH
L	HH				
M	J				J
N	JJ				JJ
	K				

still need to wear the correct band size for proper support.

Thankfully, there is no measurement needed for the shoulder straps, as they are adjustable on every bra. At least one part of this is easy!

YOUR BRA SIZE

To find the bra size you should be wearing, you'll need a tape measure (the kind you use in sewing, not the kind that comes in the tool box) to obtain the measurements we'll use to determine your band and cup sizes. You can find one at most drugstores for a couple of dollars.

Step 1: Band Size

First, wrap the tape measure around your ribcage just below your bust (be sure to exhale first) and take the measurement. Since bra band sizes are even numbers, round up to the nearest. For example, if you measure at an odd 31 inches, round up to 32.

Now comes the complicated part. The most common way of fitting advises you to add 4 inches to this number, but this method doesn't always work. Some theorize that this "old standby" fitting rule was devised

Like a Glove Fit Tip

"The secret to strapless? Always go down a bandwidth in a strapless bra for better support. If you are a 34B you would purchase a 32B." —Alicia Vargo, Pampered Passions Founder

back when bras were made with less stretch, before more pliable fabrics and materials were invented, and as a result, women who use this method often end up in bras with band sizes that are too big to offer them the proper support. What works better for many women is to add only 2 inches to their rounded-up ribcage measurement. So if you measure at 30 inches, you are likely a 32 band size.

Some fitting methods actually combine these two, advising that if your ribcage measurement is a 32 or below, then add 4 inches, and if it's a 34 or above, add only 2. And still other fitters will advise you not to add any additional inches at

49

Difference Bust Measurement Minus Band Size	U.S. Cup Size
Less than 1"	AA
1"	A
2"	B
3"	C
4"	D
5"	DD/E
6"	DDD/F
7"	G
7.5"	GG
8"	G, H
9"	H, I
10"	H, I, J
11"	HH
11.5" – 13"	I
13" – 15.5"	J
15.5" – 17"	K, JJ

In sizes above a D (and especially above a DD), there can be significant variation between brands in the number of inches difference indicated by each cup size. Use this chart for general guidance only!

all—which does work for some women. For example, I measure at a 34, and that is the band size I wear.

So what should you do? Pick whatever method you feel fits you best for now, but treat the size you get as a starting point only. Be prepared to go up or down in band size (and recalculate your cup size accordingly) to find that perfect fit. Use your size as a guideline and be sure to try on bras before you buy.

Step 2: Cup Size

Next, wrap the tape measure around the fullest part of your bust. Then subtract your band size from this number, and use the difference in inches to calculate your cup size using the chart to the left. For example, if your bust measurement is an inch larger than your band size, your cup size will most likely be an A; if your bust measurement is two inches larger than your band size, your cup size will most likely be a B; and so on.

Step 3: Try and Buy

Finally, try out your new size. Go to the store and grab various bras in the size you have measured for yourself. If you're above a DD, chances are you will have to shop online, as many stores don't carry above this size. Make sure to pick a store with a great return policy so you can still try your new size out before committing to buy.

So many women make the mistake of approaching bra shopping as if they're going grocery shopping or taking their car for an oil change. They go to the store, pluck their "size" from the rack, and buy it, expecting it to fit like a glove, only to be disappointed when they return home and find it doesn't. Think about it—would you buy a pair of shoes without trying them on? And those are just for your feet!

In bras, as in any article of clothing, so-called "standard" sizes can vary. For example, you're used to wearing a certain size, such as a size 10. But often, you'll go to the store to try on a dress or a pair of pants and end up going home with a size 12. We're not used to thinking that way when it comes to bras, but we should be.

"You can be three different sizes in a bra," says Alicia Vargo, founder of lingerie company Pampered Passions. "Just like a

Like a Glove Fit Tip

If you opt to order online, as many people do, be sure that the store has a good return policy and that you are familiar with it before you order. (One website I frequent requires that tags still be attached when you return, and I have this habit of ripping them off immediately, making them nonreturnable.)

51

pair of blue jeans or a favorite shirt, you can be many different sizes depending on who makes the bra and how their sizing system works. We have all been trained that size comes first and matters most, when in essence it's the fit of a brand that matters first and foremost." Bras fit differently depending on the manufacturer, and both band and cup sizes can be a bit off. If you got fitted at Victoria's Secret,

Fitting Uneven Breasts

....

What do you do if one of your breasts is larger (or smaller) than the other? This is a very common problem for many women; on average, women have one breast that's about half a cup size bigger than the other. But just because it's common doesn't mean it's always easy to fix. Surgery is one available option, but a more short-term solution is to fit your bra cup to the larger breast and then add some light padding to the cup on the smaller breast. Pre-surgery, I used to buy bras with removable pads and simply remove the pad on the side that was larger. Also, be sure to tighten the strap a little more on the side with the larger breast—you want to make sure it's as supported as possible.

Like a Glove Fit Tip

If you find a bra you really like but it's a bit off in the fit, you can usually get it "customized" for just a few dollars. Some stores have a seamstress on hand who will tailor your purchases for a truly perfect fit, or you can always take a trip to the neighborhood tailor. (Believe me, there is nothing to be embarrassed about. Most likely, they have altered bras before.)

you may require a different size altogether when you're at a department store trying on their brands.

Moral of the story? Try on each and every bra you want to buy *before* you leave the store. I suggest finding the style and size that you feel most comfortable in and stocking up. But it's important to note that even if you find a brand you like, different styles *within* that brand may vary, too—so you still need to try on any bra you're planning to buy. Only go bra shopping when you have at least an hour to spare and try, try, try! I know, you're busy, but aren't your "girls" important?

According to Tara Cavosie, trying before you buy is *the* most important step. "Here's the bottom line: when you are looking for a bra you really have to get in there and try on everything and see what works for you. It's not an exact science. . . . It's all about trial and error."

53

Step 1

Step 2

Step 3

Step 4

How to Put Your Bra On

It's also important to know how to properly *put on* your bra. Even if you have the right size, a bra may not fit properly because your breasts are not sitting correctly in the cups and the straps aren't adjusted the way they should be. So what's the proper way to put on a bra? It's a simple four-step process, as described by Eveden fit expert Frederika Zappe:

Step 1: Bend over till you are almost touching your toes, so that all of your breast tissue falls forward.

Step 2: Staying bent over, slip the straps over your shoulders and then hook the band on the tightest notch that is comfortable (you should still be able to fit one or two fingers between the band and your body).

Step 3: Put your hand underneath each breast and "scoop" it toward the middle and into the bra's cup (this is called the "swoop and scoop"!). This ensures your breasts are properly settled into the cups.

Step 4: Stand up and adjust the straps if necessary!

Remember that you'll likely have to adjust the shoulder straps every time you put the bra on, since wearing or washing can affect your straps' "setting."

How You Can Tell That It Fits

Here's what a proper-fitting bra looks like:

FROM THE FRONT

Underwire lies flat against the ribcage, and rests on bone (not breast tissue) on both sides

Breast tissue is perfectly settled into the *cups* so that there is no bulging or gaping

56

Bridge lies flat between the breasts

FROM THE BACK

Back of *band* is straight across and not riding up or squeezing flesh

Straps lie perfectly in place without digging in

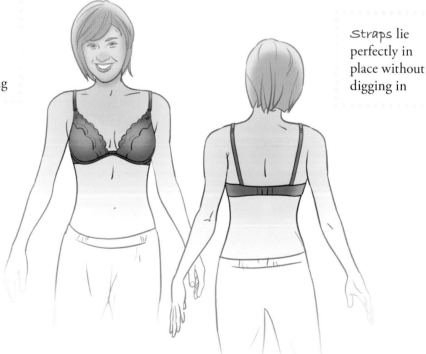

Like a Glove Fit Tip: The Perfect Bra In Under 3 Minutes!

Finding the right bra online can be tough, especially given the importance of trying on. But Zafu (www.zafu.com) aims to make the process a little easier. Just log onto the site and click on the "Bra" tab. Answer a short series of very specific questions related to breast shape, bra fit, feel, and size, and the site will recommend the "perfect" bras for you that you can order right then and there. It's sort of like a Match.com for bras!

You can also determine if your bra is fitting properly by checking where your breasts are sitting in relation to the rest of your upper body. If they are being supported correctly, the fullest part of your breasts should be positioned halfway between your shoulder and your elbow.

Alicia Vargo offers a few more tips for ensuring you've found a good fit:

Comfort is Key. Make sure it feels comfortable when you sit down and when you move your arms up, over your head, and sideways.

Looks Are Important, Too! Always try bras on while wearing a t-shirt—it's the best way to see what a bra is doing (or not doing) for you. Every bit of lace, boning, underwire, and seam can make a difference in the way you look in your bra, and under the barest t-shirt each one will show clearly. (This is also a good way to check for back and side "bulges" and other maladies.)

The Perfect Fit. Your breasts should feel like they are "sitting" upright in the cups. You should not feel any underwire pinching and your bra should feel comfortable and supportive.

Now that you've mastered your everyday bra's fit, it's time to delve into a special case: the sports bra.

Like a Glove Fit Tip

Most bra fitters recommend you fit your bra so that it hooks comfortably on the middle hook, allowing you to extend to an outside hook if you gain a little weight, and an inside hook if you lose some or the band stretches.

58

SPORTS SUPPORT

Sports bras have been around for thirty years yet are still a mystery to most women. But proper fit and support is just as important in a sports bra as in the everyday model—maybe more! Researchers say an unsupported breast can move up and down about six centimeters when we're working out. Not a good thing for the girls.

Whether you're a jogger, a dancer, a kickboxer, or a yoga enthusiast, you need a well-fitting sports bra that keeps your breasts firmly in place when you move— even if you're a small-breasted woman! Actress Katie Holmes raised eyebrows when she appeared to be braless while running the New York City marathon. It's always a good idea to support any and all breast tissue with a proper-fitting sports bra, even if you feel like you don't need it.

Sports bras generally come in two basic designs: *Compression* and *Encapsulation*. Sound scientific? Well, they are. These "models" have been developed as a result of research like the study from Chapter 2, and each is designed to minimize movement of the breasts in a different way. When you wear the compression style, the most common type of sports bra, your breasts are pressed together, flat against your chest, to reduce motion. This option best suits

Compression

Encapsulation

60

smaller-breasted women (up to a D-cup) as compression sports bras can often be too "constraining," and less effective, for larger-breasted women. Compression-style bras come sized small, medium, or large. Usually, a small correlates to a 32B/C, a medium to a 34B/C, and a large to a 36B/C. If you are an A, try on the small. If you are a D or larger, try a large or extra-large. In some cases, the extra-large won't be big enough, so you'll want to look for a sports bra that comes

in your exact band and cup size—like an encapsulation-style sports bra.

Encapsulation sports bras are sized like regular bras, by both band and cup size. According to a 2006 article by Thomas Affatato on www.infinitehealthresources.com, "encapsulation models are constructed with two cups (just like typical bras), under the theory that two small masses are easier to control than one large one." Experts say this is the better option for women whose breasts are larger than a D-cup, as this type offers more support by compressing each breast separately.

If you're in the store, you can usually tell which style is which. Compression bras are usually one piece and designed to be pulled on over your head, whereas encapsulation bras have actual "cups" and often an underwire as well. Keep in mind that, no matter which style you choose, sports bras are meant to feel snugger than your normal bra, but they shouldn't be so tight that they irritate your skin.

Sports bras are infamous for creating a uniboob appearance (especially the compression models) but many on the market today are much more flattering. Plus, many sports bras are even chic enough to wear by themselves! You'll stay cooler in them that way, too. I have taken a liking to a style by Nike that zips up in the front—you can adjust your breast tissue after you zip it up and create great cleavage, sans uniboob effect. But whichever style you choose, it's important to shop around and get the best fit you can.

> ### Like a Glove Fit Tip
> Your sports bra's tag can be a wealth of information. In addition to listing size and material, sometimes it even tells you what activities the bra is designed for.

Here are some tips for finding a great-fitting sports bra:

61

- ▶ Make sure the elastic band on the bottom fits snugly around your ribcage, but not so snugly that you can't breathe.

- ▶ Jump up and down a few times in the dressing room. You may look a little crazy, but you'll accurately determine if the bra gives you the amount of support needed for physical activity! Obviously, the less "bounce," the better. The sports bra, more than any other bra, is all about limiting range of motion.

Like a Glove Fast Fact

A Harris survey commissioned by Playtex asked more than 1,000 women what they like in a bra. Sixty-seven percent said they prefer wearing a bra over going braless. Eighty-five percent said they want a "shape-enhancing bra that feels like nothing at all." On the issue of underwire, ladies were split. Forty-nine percent said they prefer underwire while 49 percent said they prefer to do without.

▶ Look for wider shoulder straps for increased support.

▶ Note that those with built-in "shock absorbers" are designed to minimize bounce.

The fabric you choose also has an impact on the comfort and effectiveness of the sports bra—most are designed to wick moisture away from the body, but you can choose one that also goes a step further by preventing chafing and all-around discomfort. Check the tag before you buy so you know what your sports bra is made of.

According to www.olympiasports.net, there are several different fabrics to choose from. Here is a breakdown of the options, with the most common first:

Polyester/Cotton: This classic blend provides gentle softness and powerful moisture management for all your workouts.

Cotton/Lycra: This combination of soft, moisture-managing cotton and shape-retaining Lycra creates a very comfortable fabric with just the right amount of stretch and support.

Making an Impact

Different activities have different impacts on our bodies (and our breasts), so many sports bras are designed with that in mind. Here is a guideline so you know what type of sports bra to look for, depending on the activity:

Low Impact	Medium Impact	High Impact
Walking	Skiing	Aerobics
Yoga	Skating	Running
Bicycling	Tennis	Mountain biking
Weight training	Golf	Softball
Low-impact aerobics		Soccer
		Basketball
		Horseback riding
		Kickboxing/boxing

CoolMax polyester/Lycra: This high-performance fabric blend delivers you all the moisture-wicking benefits of CoolMax plus the comfort, stretch, and shape retention of Lycra.

Polyester/Cotton/Lycra: This three-fiber blend offers polyester and cotton for softness and moisture management while Lycra provides optimal fit and support.

Supplex nylon/Lycra: This blend offers soft, luxurious feel and incredible fit, support, and shape retention.

Because of wear and tear, sports bras should also be replaced at least every year, depending on how much use they get. How do you know if it's time for a new one? Tell-tale signs are if the elastic is stretched out and no longer flush against your ribcage or if you notice increased breast motion or pilling on the fabric.

Bra Fit Cheat Sheet

Just to recap, here are the three most important points to remember when it comes to bra fit:

▶ *See a Pro.* Seeing a professional for measurements will help ensure you figure out the correct size. A professional can also help you weave your way through the maze of brassieres that promise to lift, separate, and even mimic a boob job!

▶ *Don't Get Stuck in a Size-Rut.* You need to get re-fitted every six months to a year! Our breasts are constantly changing as we age and gain or lose weight, and especially after giving birth.

▶ *Try Before You Buy.* Bra sizes run differently depending on the brand, so even after you get fitted, you still need to try yours on to make sure it fits!

four

Going Undercover

Bras and Fashion

Fit isn't the only important factor when choosing the right bra. Many of our bra decisions revolve around fashion, as well. In fact, a survey by market research firm NPD Group showed that 66 percent of women choose the style and color of bra based on the clothes they'll be wearing.

Whether you're dressing for a special occasion or just for everyday life, you need to start with what's underneath! Bras are the first layer of your outfit and can have a huge effect on your overall appearance. "Creating the perfect foundation for your clothes is just as important as finding the perfect outfit," says Spanx founder Sara Blakely. Pick the right one—and your girls will look great no matter what you are wearing. (Disclaimer: We take no responsibility for that latex tube top.)

Just like you have different clothes for different occasions—like casual for the weekends, business for weekdays, and eveningwear for special events—you need different bras to meet different wardrobe needs. It would look really strange if you wore a push-up bra while working out, wouldn't it?

You should have a full arsenal of bras to fit your lifestyle, and in this chapter, we are going to present all the options. That way, you can decide for yourself what you need, based on the clothes in your closet.

Bra Wardrobe Basics

....

According to Cyla Weiner, owner of Sylene, a lingerie store in Washington, D.C., "[every] woman should have at least seven different types of bras, one for each day of the week." Weiner uses a guideline that she calls the "s-factor": Each necessary bra begins with the letter "s." These seven staples serve as the foundation for your bra rotation:

▶ One "Strapless" bra. The strapless bra is not just for eveningwear anymore. A strapless bra can be the one you use the most, especially if you get one that fits like a glove and is convertible—has removable straps—that allow you to wear it in a variety of ways, with a variety of outfits.

▶ One "Spa" bra, for everyday comfort. T-shirt bras and contour bras fall into this category.

▶ One "Specialty" bra, such as a plunge bra, for low-front tops and dresses.

▶ One "Sports" bra.

▶ Three "Sexy" bras, for evening, special occasions, and everyday work attire. This includes at least one demi-cup or balconette bra (for lower-cut tops) and at least one sheer or lacy (or whatever defines sexy to you!) full-coverage bra,

Bra Fashion Fast Fact

The bra wasn't always a wardrobe staple. Women didn't begin wearing them regularly until the early 1900s. At that time, bras were used to retain breasts, not enhance them, and women certainly weren't looking at them as a fashion item. By 1918, however, bras had become a fashion basic, and more than fifty different brands were available through department stores, in a plethora of styles.

for higher-cut tops. Note that demi cups are most flattering on small to medium busts, so if you have larger breasts you may want to look for some pretty full-coverage styles instead. Conversely, a smaller-busted woman may want to skip the full-coverage option and opt for a push-up instead!

Keep in mind, you'll want to adjust these recommendations for your own personal bra needs. If you are in casual wear the majority of the time, you'll want to stock up more on "Spa" bras, whereas a woman who spends 90 percent of her time in blouses and suits will want more of the dressier bras.

71

What to Wear *Under* There

Now that you know what bras you should have, you need to know what to wear them with. Knowing what goes under what can help you avert a major wardrobe malfunction.

Here is *The Bra Book*'s guide to what to wear under what (and if you need a little help on what each type of bra is, refer back to our bra alphabet in Chapter 2!).

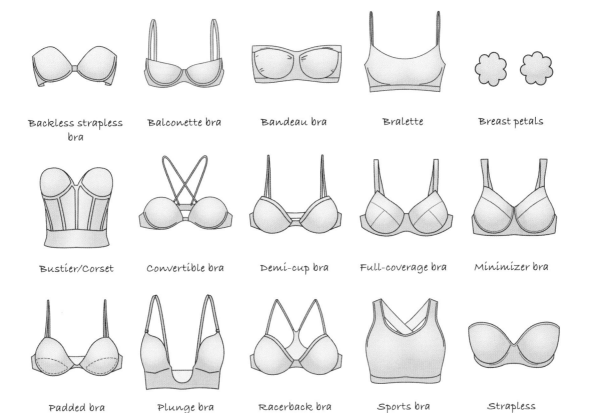

Backless strapless bra

Balconette bra

Bandeau bra

Bralette

Breast petals

Bustier/Corset

Convertible bra

Demi-cup bra

Full-coverage bra

Minimizer bra

Padded bra

Plunge bra

Racerback bra

Sports bra

Strapless

Support adhesives

T-shirt bra

KEY

EVERYDAY

T-shirt or clingy top		A bra that's seamless, soft, and molded will stay invisible under thin fabric.
Sheer top		Unless you want the bra to show through, make sure it's nude-colored!
Deep v-neck sweater		
Low-cut top		Which bra is best will depend on the cut of the top.
Backless or low-back top		Look for a convertible bra where the band is also a strap that can wrap around the waist.
Boat neck top		
Off-the-shoulder top		
Tank top		
Sleeveless top		
Strapless top		

SPECIAL OCCASIONS

Gown or dress
with spaghetti straps

Halter dress or gown

You may need a convertible plunge
bra in some cases, depending on
how deep the neckline is.

One-shoulder
dress or gown

Wear one strap diagonally over the
covered shoulder.

Strapless
dress or gown

Which bra is best will depend on
the style of the dress.

Corset-style
dress or gown

Or go braless! This style usually
has enough structure to support
you on its own.

75

Dress or gown with a
plunging neckline

Backless
dress or gown

Dress or gown
that plunges in both front
and back

Dress or gown with a
strappy back and a sheer
or revealed midriff area

> **Bra Fashion Fast Fact**
>
> Corsets, the pain-inducing predecessors of the bra, were once used by women as a means of attaining a pushed-up bosom and an unnaturally small waist. Now, corset styles are back in the fashion spotlight—less as a waist-cincher than a decorative accessory—gracing everything from evening gowns to blouses.

Although these charts cover nearly every clothing style imaginable, sometimes you have to wear something and the bra you need just doesn't exist. Take this scenario, for example: Your friend asks you to be a bridesmaid in her wedding. She chooses the dress, and it's completely complicated. You give it a good eyeballing and know right off the bat it's not going to work with any of the bras you own—or any bra you've ever *seen*, for that matter. And it's not like you can just decide to *not* wear that dress. So what's the solution?

Bra designer Tara Cavosie was in this exact same situation when she created the Backless Strapless Bra, which is made by Fashion Forms. But those of us who aren't quite as crafty can visit our local tailor. With a little snipping and some creative sewing, a seamstress can customize your bra exactly to your dress. Keep in mind, you should never sew your bra *into* your gown; as you move, *it* can move, and both bra and dress can end up looking pretty strange. However, seamstresses say sewn-in bra cups do work better for people whose cup sizes are smaller than a C, since things are less likely to shift out of place.

COLOR-CODING

Technically a bra is underwear, which means it's not meant to be *seen* under your clothes. But the color bra you choose is still important. For one thing, your bra's color can greatly determine its visibility. You want your bra to go unnoticed . . . unless you're Madonna, or just very daring (but hey, that's your prerogative).

Follow the chart on the next page to determine what you can wear with each color bra. But first, two important rules regarding bra color:

In the Buff: You need at least two nude- or flesh-colored bras. (Why two? So you

Bra Fashion Fast Fact

Does your bra have to always match your panties? According to an Agent Provocateur poll on FabSugar (www.fabsugar. com), 55 percent of respondents say, "No!" Women polled by Shopsmart.org (www. shopsmart.org) agreed—58 percent said they never or rarely play the matching game.

can rotate, or in case one is in the wash!) Contrary to popular belief, it's a nude bra that's the most versatile, not a white one. A white bra is fine for dark colors and thicker fabrics, but it usually shows under white tops. The nude bra, on the other hand, is inconspicuous under just about *everything*. And bras come in different shades of tan, beige, and brown, so you can find a perfect match regardless of your skin tone. In my eyes, you can never have enough nude bras!

Black is Back: You also need at least two black bras for wearing under darker clothing, especially black. A nude bra, especially the edges of the cups, can show through black if the sweater or top is at all sheer. In cases like this, a plain black bra will work better.

BRA COLOR	TOP OR DRESS COLOR
NUDE	Wear under any and every color, and the sheerest of fabrics!
WHITE	Wear under colors only. Do not wear under white!
BLACK	Wear under black/navy.
BRIGHT COLORS	Wear under black/navy/other bright colors.
PATTERNED/LACE/ MULTI-COLORED	Wear under black/navy/other bright colors. (*Caution*: If the color is dark but the fabric is thin or sheer, you may need a nude or less textured bra instead.)

A BRA FOR EVERY BODY TYPE

Your outfit shouldn't be the only thing flattering your figure. Your bra should be figure-flattering, too! The right bra can help create a more balanced silhouette under clothes. The first step, though, is knowing just what your "figure" is.

While there are many different theories for classifying female figures, for our purposes we'll use a common guideline that outlines four basic body types:

◄ *Apple or upside-down triangle.* Women with this body type tend to store fat around the midsection, making them rounder in the middle like an apple and creating a body shape that's broader on the top and narrower on the bottom like an upside-down triangle.

▶ *Hourglass.* Women with this body type look like hourglasses: evenly proportioned on top and bottom, with noticeable narrowing at the waist.

79

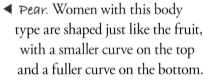

Bra Fashion Fast Fact

A 2005 study by researchers at North Carolina State University found that even though only about 8 percent of women are hourglass-shaped, clothing designers and manufacturers were still building clothes based on a slim version of that body type. Of the 6,000 women studied, nearly half were rectangles while just over 20 percent were pear-shaped. About 14 percent were apples or inverted triangles.

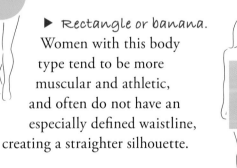

◀ Pear. Women with this body type are shaped just like the fruit, with a smaller curve on the top and a fuller curve on the bottom.

▶ Rectangle or banana. Women with this body type tend to be more muscular and athletic, and often do not have an especially defined waistline, creating a straighter silhouette.

Most women fall into one of these categories.

Certain bras enhance certain shapes better than others. The key is to choose a bra that evens out your proportions. For example, if you're larger on top, like an apple or upside-down triangle, you may want to look for a minimizing bra. If you're larger on the bottom, like a pear, you may want to look for a push-up bra with a little padding to balance out your wider hips.

In the chart on the next page, note your body type and what kind of bras you should be looking for.

BODY TYPE	WHAT TO LOOK FOR/ WHAT TO AVOID
Apple/ Inverted Triangle	Look For: minimizing bras (which will deemphasize your larger bust) Avoid: push-up and padded bras (which make you look even larger on top)
Hourglass	You can wear almost any bra; lucky you! But you might want to look for something that enhances your cleavage and further accentuates your hourglass shape.
Pear	Look For: push-up and padded bras (which will go a long way in balancing out your ample hips) Avoid: bralettes and minimizing bras (which compress and deemphasize your breasts)
Banana/Rectangle	Look For: cleavage-enhancing bra with wide-set straps, like balconettes (which will narrow your shoulders and feminize your figure) Avoid: minimizing bras or compression type sports bras (which will make your shoulders and chest appear broader)

To sum up what we've learned in this chapter: Make note of your body type, stock up on black and nude bras, opt for versatile styles that will take you from a day at the office to your best friend's wedding with just a switch of the straps, and while comfort is key, don't forget to snag a few sexy styles, too. You'll be sure to have the right bra for every occasion—and every outfit!

five

Your Bra

and

Your Body

REMEMBER THE FAMOUS BROOKE SHIELDS COMMERCIAL WHERE SHE proclaimed, "Nothing gets between me and my Calvins"? Forget jeans. Nothing gets between you and your bra, literally. It's the closest thing to your body at all times . . . and the article of clothing that's perhaps *most* affected by changes to your body.

Our bodies don't look the same at ten as they do at forty, so why would our breasts? According to a study of 500 women conducted by www.myintimacy.com, the average woman's breasts will "change shape, size, and distribution at least six times during the course of her life." Our breasts are constantly changing. Though the most dramatic changes tend to occur at puberty, we experience a bevy of body changes throughout our lifetimes that can affect what we need from our bras. That's why it's important to understand what these changes are, and how our breasts can support us through them, both physically and emotionally.

In this chapter, we'll look at seven common changes our breasts go through:

- ▶ Puberty
- ▶ Pregnancy and breastfeeding
- ▶ Weight loss or gain
- ▶ Mastectomy
- ▶ Breast augmentation and other surgery to the breasts
- ▶ Menstrual cycle, menopause, and other hormonal fluctuations
- ▶ Aging

PUBERTY

· ·

At the onset of puberty—generally between the ages of nine and sixteen—a girl typically gets her period, starts to grow body hair, and begins to develop breasts. She'll often also start wearing a bra during this time, even if she doesn't yet have a whole lot to put in it.

Whether because it's more socially acceptable (all her friends are wearing one) or her breasts have actually begun to develop, you'll want to get her what's typically known as a "training bra." Training bras come in sizes that are smaller than an A-cup (such as AAA and AA), and are generally wireless and made of comfortable, stretchy fabrics such as cotton blends. For young girls who are blossoming a bit larger right off the bat, you may want to skip directly to a soft-cup bra such as the CC Girl Seamless Pull-Over Day Bra, which is made specifically for girls who are going through puberty (you can find it at www.dotgirlproducts. com, a site that caters to and educates about a girl's firsts: first periods, first bras, and more!). A compression-style sports bra, which comes in sizes small, medium, and large, is also a suitable alternative to a training bra. You can use your child's clothing sizes as a guideline.

Your Bra and Your Body Tit-Bit

A girl's relationship with bras starts earlier now than it did thirty years ago. Published reports cite research that indicates girls are hitting puberty and developing breasts (and shopping for training bras) one to two years earlier than their moms did.

If you have a pre-teen or teen who is about to go through puberty or who is currently in the middle of it, be sure to help her through this process by educating her and supporting her as much as she needs. Mistakes in a girl's early bra-wearing days can be very damaging to her emotional health. As a teenager, I was mocked in school for not wearing a bra when everyone else had already begun wearing one, and then a year or so later, for wearing my favorite pink bra under a sheer white shirt. It's something I still remember as an adult!

The best way to help her through this important milestone is to take her to a department store or lingerie store for an expert bra fitting (and while you're at it, get one for yourself, too!). She will have to do this many more times in her life, so this will help her become comfortable with it early on and alleviate the embarrassment factor as she grows and matures.

88

"When your child is twelve, your wife buys her a splendidly silly article of clothing called a training bra. To train what? I never had a training jock and believe me, when I played football, I could have used a training jock more than any twelve-year-old needs a training bra."
– Bill Cosby

PREGNANCY AND BREASTFEEDING

Pregnancy, quite possibly the biggest milestone in a woman's life, also takes the biggest toll on her body—including her breasts. The rapid weight gain and loss and the breastfeeding that often follows can cause everything from sagging to volume loss. "Predicting how a woman's breasts will change with pregnancy is a task for a genie with a crystal ball," says Dr. Garth Fisher, renowned Beverly Hills plastic surgeon, *Extreme Makeover* star, and author of the DVD series *The Naked Truth about Plastic Surgery*. "In general, pregnancy and nursing will cause the breast to engorge, stretch, and [then] droop or deflate."

The breasts are often the first part of the body to be affected by pregnancy, and your bra size—and type of bra you need—will inevitably change, both during and after pregnancy. According to "The New Moms' Nursing Bra Guide," an article on www.ezinearticles.com, during pregnancy and breastfeeding, women generally go up at least one band size *and* one cup size, thanks to swollen breasts and a ribcage that's growing to accommodate your growing baby. Some women have reported going through dozens of bras in those nine months alone. During my first pregnancy, which occurred while I was

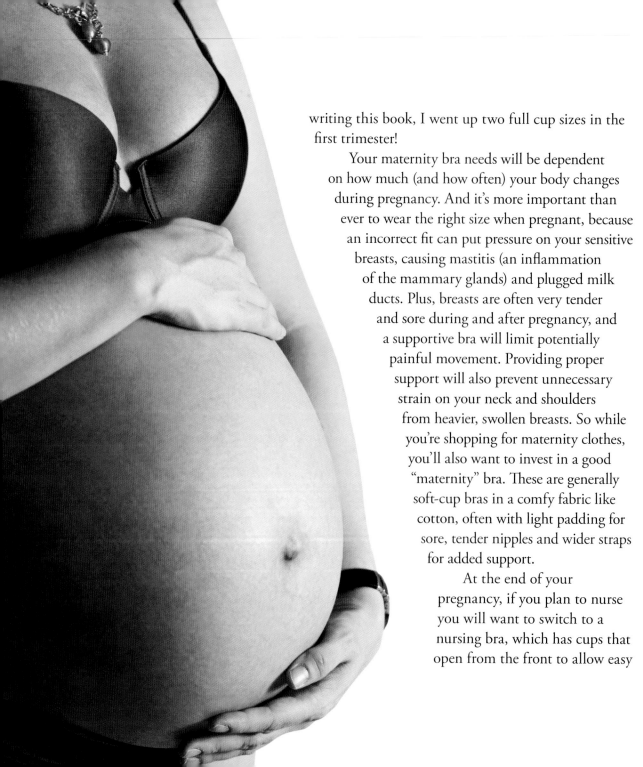

writing this book, I went up two full cup sizes in the first trimester!

Your maternity bra needs will be dependent on how much (and how often) your body changes during pregnancy. And it's more important than ever to wear the right size when pregnant, because an incorrect fit can put pressure on your sensitive breasts, causing mastitis (an inflammation of the mammary glands) and plugged milk ducts. Plus, breasts are often very tender and sore during and after pregnancy, and a supportive bra will limit potentially painful movement. Providing proper support will also prevent unnecessary strain on your neck and shoulders from heavier, swollen breasts. So while you're shopping for maternity clothes, you'll also want to invest in a good "maternity" bra. These are generally soft-cup bras in a comfy fabric like cotton, often with light padding for sore, tender nipples and wider straps for added support.

At the end of your pregnancy, if you plan to nurse you will want to switch to a nursing bra, which has cups that open from the front to allow easy access for breastfeeding. There are four different types of nursing bras, each one providing a different method for allowing the baby access to your breast. The first fastens between the cups in the front. The second has zippers that sit under each cup. The third fastens at the straps, allowing you to pull the cups down. The last has a crossover design in the front that allows you to just slip your breast out. Just choose the design that you will be most comfortable with!

If you want to buy your nursing bras before your baby is born, keep in mind that within a few days of giving birth, your breasts will swell due to milk production, so the bras you choose should be able to comfortably stretch to accommodate that. According to ConsumerReports.org (www.consumerreports.org), the best nursing bras are "stretchy, absorbent, and don't bind the breasts in any way that could interfere with milk flow. Look for bras that are 100% cotton or a cotton-Lycra blend or other stretchy synthetic."

When choosing the proper size and fit, you should follow the guidelines outlined in Chapter 3. A professional

> ### Your Bra and Your Body Tit-Bit
>
> If during pregnancy your band is getting too tight but the cups are still fitting well, you can try Fashion Forms' Soft Back Bra Extenders. They hook on to the back of your current bras to add inches of comfort.

91

fitting is recommended here, too, although in many hospitals the lactation consultant you are given during your stay is also equipped to do this. "The New Moms' Nursing Bra Guide" recommends a bra that has several hooks so you can just switch to a tighter hook once your ribcage goes back to its normal size after you give birth. (According to What to Expect [www.whattoexpect.com], about six weeks post-delivery, your band size will likely go back down to what it was pre-pregnancy, though you may remain about a cup size larger. Everyone is different!) The Body Silk Seamless Nursing Bra by Bravado! Designs is actually designed to fit several band and cup sizes to allow for your body's fluctuations during this time.

During breastfeeding, you may want to avoid bras that have an underwire, as one that is too tight can restrict the milk ducts and cause serious complications. In the absence of an underwire, however, the straps and cups will end up taking on more of the support responsibilities, so look for a bra with wider straps and consider investing in attachable shoulder strap pads, like Fashion Forms' Comfy Shoulder, to alleviate any digging in. You may also want to opt for a nursing bra with some slight padding. I have friends who

92

have learned the hard way that, otherwise, milk can leak from your breasts and cause some embarrassment when you're wearing a thin top.

When trying on a nursing bra, you'll want to not only check for comfort and fit but also whether the cups are easy to open when you have your hungry newborn in your arms. You'll have plenty of options to choose from (ConsumerReports.org did a review of several of them), including athletic styles that are extra supportive, styles for sleeping in, and even some built into tank tops. For the best selection of maternity and nursing bras, visit stores with inventory especially for expectant moms, like the national chain Destination Maternity (their staff is also trained in fitting).

WEIGHT GAIN OR LOSS

When you gain weight, your breasts can stretch and grow along with the rest of your body. When you lose weight, your breasts may lose volume, too. Every woman's body is different: Some women don't lose any weight at all in their breasts when they drop pounds, making their breasts seem proportionately larger, and others lose weight in their breasts first. The best thing to do after any shift in weight is get re-fitted; even if the volume of your breasts hasn't changed, your band size may have!

Changes in weight can cause more than just changes in breast size. When you gain and then lose weight, your skin—

which has stretched to accommodate the additional weight—may still be stretched out. In the breasts, this can result in a decrease in fullness and firmness. A push-up or padded bra, or the use of cutlets, can aid in giving the appearance of volume and firmness back to your breasts.

POST-MASTECTOMY

Unfortunately, most of us know someone who has had to undergo a breast removal procedure, or mastectomy. This is usually done as a treatment for (or in some cases for the prevention of) breast cancer, which 1 in 8 women will get in her lifetime, according to American Cancer Society statistics.

If you have to undergo a mastectomy, whether or not the procedure involves an immediate reconstruction, you will generally want to purchase a special post-mastectomy bra (though women should wear post-surgical garments for six to eight weeks after surgery before switching to even a post-mastectomy bra). Post-mastectomy bras are usually made of soft, breathable cotton, have specially designed straps to prevent "cup bounce," and are adjustable for ease of movement and to keep from irritating the surgery site. While these bras are often designed with pockets to hold breast forms, or prostheses, in place, a pocketed bra is not absolutely necessary. The benefit of a pocketed bra is that it helps absorb moisture between the chest and breast form and also keeps the prosthesis from slipping out of place.

Some companies are going an extra step to make post-surgical bras more comfortable for women. Amoena's Hanna Collection is one of the industry's first to offer camisoles and bras infused with vitamin E and aloe to ease discomfort and promote healing after breast surgery. The company also has specially trained fit specialists on hand to help breast cancer patients find the best bra to meet their needs at www.amoena.com.

Some women undergo post-mastectomy breast reconstruction through the use of "tissue expanders," which are temporary saline implants placed at the site or sites where breast tissue is removed. Through a series of doctor's visits over several months, saline is pumped into the implant, gradually stretching the skin. In this case, you might wear a different bra size through every stage of the expansion, so be prepared to get re-fitted every time.

Vera Garofalo, post-mastectomy expert and program manager of Hope's Boutique at the James Cancer Hospital and Solove Research Institute in Dublin, Ohio, strongly recommends visiting a mastectomy fitter who has been certified by the American Board for Certification in Orthotics,

Your Bra and Your Body Tit-Bit

Early detection of breast cancer can not only prevent you from having to undergo a mastectomy, it can also save your life. The American Cancer Society says women over forty should have a mammogram—an X-ray of the breast—every year. Women at high risk (those with a family history or who have been diagnosed with the so-called "breast cancer gene") should start screening as early as age thirty. It's also important to do monthly self-exams at home so if you feel any unusual lumps you can bring them to the attention of your doctor.

95

Woman getting fitted for a post-mastectomy bra.

Prosthetics, and Pedorthics. You can find one near you by visiting their website at www.abcop.org/Mastectomy_Fitter.asp.

96

Meanwhile, here are Vera's tips for shopping for post-mastectomy bras:

▶ The band of the bra should hook so it fits comfortably snug just like with a regular bra. Having the correct band size is especially important to prevent the bra from shifting or riding up, since this can dislodge or displace the prosthesis. You are trying to simulate the natural breast, which, unlike the prosthesis, is attached to your body and cannot move. Also, when the prosthesis does not stay secure, it can cause rubbing at the surgery site, causing extra sensitivity, and continually pulling at your bra if it is shifting or riding up will only increase that discomfort.

▶ The straps should be adjusted so that each breast and/or prosthesis is held securely and at a comfortable level. Straps should fit snugly without cutting into the shoulders; you should be able to get one finger under the strap. You may want to look for padded straps for added comfort or opt for separate, attachable strap pads. The prosthesis will inevitably differ in weight from the natural breast, and adjusting the straps is crucial for achieving symmetry and keeping the prosthesis secure.

▶ The cup should fit smoothly and completely cover the breast tissue

and surgical area. For optimum comfort, it should hug the chest without any gaping.

Of course, any and all options and care for post surgery should be discussed with and monitored by your doctor.

BREAST AUGMENTATION AND OTHER SURGERY TO THE BREASTS

· ·

Millions of women are opting to go under the knife for bigger—or smaller—boobs. In fact, for the first time since the American Society of Plastic Surgeons began compiling statistics, breast augmentation was found to be the most popular cosmetic surgical procedure, with hundreds of thousands of women undergoing the procedure each and every year. There are also many women who opt to undergo breast reduction surgery, often because their breasts are so large or heavy that it causes them physical pain. In each case, finding the right bra afterward can involve special challenges.

If you undergo breast augmentation surgery, or an enlargement of the breasts through the use of implants, you can expect to wear a post-surgical bra for four to six weeks after surgery. In some cases, this is a compression-style bra with a strap on top that is used to push the implants downward and keep them in place. In others, you may be given a soft bra that resembles a sports bra (or an actual sports bra!) instead. Which bra you receive depends on the surgeon, the incisions, and the extent of the enlargement. Most doctors determine the best post-operative bra on a case-by-case basis. After this four- to six-week period, usually the

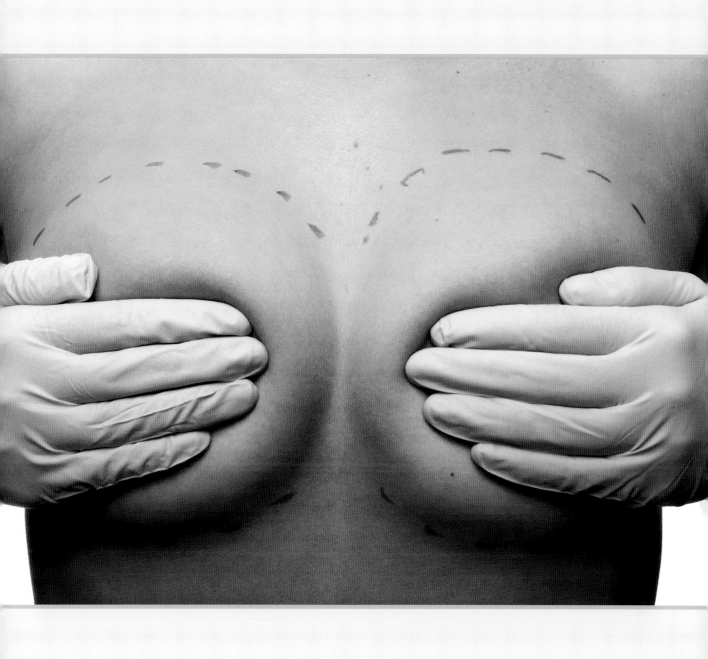

first thing you'll want to do is dash out to the lingerie store to shop for your new, improved size. But figuring out bra size isn't any easier for breast augmentation patients than it is for anyone else.

It's a misconception that your doctor can tell you your new bra size based on the size of the implants inserted. We've all heard the women on makeover shows say, "Make me a C cup," or "I want to be a D," but every doctor I've spoken to tells me this is unrealistic. Implants come in many sizes, and none of them correspond to cup size. Implant sizes are named by the volume of solution (either saline or silicone) that the implant holds, often measured in CCs, or cubic centimeters. And as we already know, cup sizes are determined in proportion to band sizes. So a doctor certainly can't tell you for sure that your new size will be a C-cup.

As always, your first step should be to get a professional fitting to determine your new size. But it's best to wait until the swelling has gone down (unless you plan on buying new bras—*again*—once it does). When this happens all depends on your body. While doctors say swelling

can start to subside in as little as two weeks, you won't be at your new true size and shape until at least six to eight weeks. For some women, it can take up to three months.

Once you have been fitted and purchased new bras, it's a good idea to take them to your doctor to make sure they won't interfere with the healing process in any way. Even after the swelling subsides, your breasts are still healing and can continue to do so for months.

Speaking of healing, if your surgery involved incisions around the nipple or an added procedure such as a breast lift that involves multiple incisions, you'll want to look for a bra in a soft, "non-scratchy" fabric like cotton so you won't risk irritating them. If your incisions are in the breast fold, as they are in many augmentations, underwire could irritate them, so you may want to stick to a bra without underwire until the incisions are completely healed.

There is a common myth that wearing a push-up or underwire bra can harm augmented breasts or cause your implants to shift. Some doctors will even argue the same. But I consulted with New York–based plastic surgeon Dr. C. Andrew Salzberg, the self-proclaimed pioneer of the One-Stage Breast Reconstruction procedure (in which women who undergo a mastectomy receive a reconstruction in the same operation), and he disputes this. "There is no reason you can't wear any bra you want and no medical proof to support claims that underwire will harm the implant," says Salzberg. "The only thing that can cause the implant to move is if the internal 'pocket' that holds the breast implant is too big or, over time, the muscle comes up, causing the implant to slide down—not a bra." Ill-fitting underwire that is not positioned properly in your breast fold and is digging into your breast tissue, however, can certainly cause pain and discomfort. Many doctors do advise avoiding underwire altogether for at least the first month or two if your surgery involved incisions in the folds of the breasts. You want to avoid anything that might rub against the incision site, because it can cause irritation and possibly make the scars worse.

One other thing to keep in mind when buying post-augmentation bras: Implants are often also wider than natural

101

"I am totally against plastic surgery. A lot of people think I have breast implants because I have the biggest boobs in the business. But I was a 34C when I was seventeen. . . . They stay up when I wear a push-up bra. But if people could see me when I come home and take off my bra, how could they think these are fake?"
– Tyra Banks

breasts, so you may need to look for a fuller-coverage cup than you're used to.

What if your surgery involved a reduction in breast size? According to Dr. Andrew Kleinman, a plastic surgeon in Rye Brook, New York, post-surgical bras for breast reduction patients don't differ that much from augmentation patients'. However, the breast reduction patient usually "will wear this bra for a week or two and then is usually able to switch to any bra that is comfortable and doesn't irritate any incision sites."

Because every reduction patient is different—every patient has a different amount of breast tissue removed, plus age, skin texture, and whether or not the patient has had children can all be factors—the number of bras you can expect to go through post-surgery is hard to predict, too. "Swelling does change over the course of a few months and the new shape of the breasts has to settle over the course of a few months, too," says Dr. Kleinman. "How long this process takes is very dependent on the surgical technique used and the patient. It is not uncommon after a substantial reduction for the size

and shape to change for up to a year." That means lots of bra fittings—and lots of bras. But, Dr. Kleinman adds, most patients will be fit into a bra that will be "fairly appropriate for the long-term" after about three months.

Perhaps the hardest thing for reduction patients to grasp is that the size of their breasts is not the only thing that will change after surgery—the shape will, too. "With a reduction, you are not just changing the size of the breasts to make them smaller; you're also restoring the position of the breast to a more normal position since women with very large breasts tend to experience a lot of sagging," Dr. Kleinman notes. So you're looking at not just size, but position and shape changes, too.

Reduction patients also have much different scarring patterns than augmentation patients. Scars can range from a small line around the areola, to a "lollipop" shape on the breast, to an "anchor" shape—which can make it more difficult to find a bra that won't irritate your incision site. "It's important to find a bra that's comfortable and doesn't irritate any of the incisions while they are healing.

Hollywood Breasts

Breasts come in all shapes and sizes, yet plastic surgeons say more and more women are asking for round, unnaturally shaped breasts. Is Hollywood to blame? "I believe the craze for 'round Hollywood breasts' started with Pamela Anderson and the *Baywatch* days," says plastic surgeon Dr. Garth Fisher. "Some of the most visualized breasts on television were round and oversized and many of the first implants were made in that shape." According to most doctors, natural breasts tend to be shaped more like a teardrop.

Today implants are being made in all shapes and sizes so a woman can have whatever she desires. Newly approved silicone implants are a popular choice and can help give breasts a more natural look and feel compared to the saline variety. There are also bras that create the much-sought "round" implant look, such as the aptly named Hollywood Extreme Cleavage Bra from Frederick's of Hollywood. Through strategically placed pads in the lower part of the cup, this bra helps push together and round out the breasts, creating a very spherical appearance and covetable cleavage.

A bra that rubs against the incision sites can cause skin sores, so you want to avoid that at all costs. That is even more important than finding the proper fit after surgery. If you can find a fit that's close enough, and it feels comfortable, then you are in the right bra."

Whether you're having a breast enlargement or a reduction, Dr. Kleinman says, you'll want to keep in mind that the shape of your breasts will change over the years in slightly different ways than natural breasts would. "Just like a woman who has larger breasts will sag faster than a woman with smaller breasts, women with breasts that have been operated on will notice different changes than those who have un-augmented breasts. Healing is not a static thing with these procedures; it's dynamic. So you'll notice that you'll be changing the style of bra you like and wear every couple of years."

Your Bra and Your Body Tit-Bit

Finally, a bra made specifically for women who have undergone breast augmentation! Bra company Le Mystère developed the No. 9 collection with the help of a board certified plastic surgeon to meet the needs of women who post-surgery were unable to find bras that fit their new breasts. The bras' cup shape is tailored to that of augmented breasts, with a wider center connector to accommodate their often wider cleavage. You can find the No. 9 collection at select department stores or online at www.pamperedpassions.com.

Menstrual Cycle, Menopause, and Other Hormonal Fluctuations

Ah, hormones. They are always messing everything up for us gals, right? And we have to deal with them not just during puberty, pregnancy, and menopause, but each and every month!

There are plenty of reasons your hormones can fluctuate (two of which—puberty and pregnancy—we've talked about already), but let's start with the most frequent: your period. During your period, swelling breasts can cause your bra size to increase up to one full cup size! Accordingly, it's good to keep at least one bra on hand that's a bit more "full coverage" to accommodate this change.

You may even want to purchase a bra or two specifically for that one week out of the month. Many women I know also switch to a bra with softer cups during this time to avoid irritating sensitive nipples.

Perhaps the biggest hormonal changes happen during menopause. Between hot flashes, decreased sex drive, and other menopausal symptoms, you also have to deal with changing breasts. According to the National Cancer Institute, "when you stop having periods at the onset of menopause, your hormone levels drop, and your breast tissue becomes less dense and more fatty." This can lead to increased

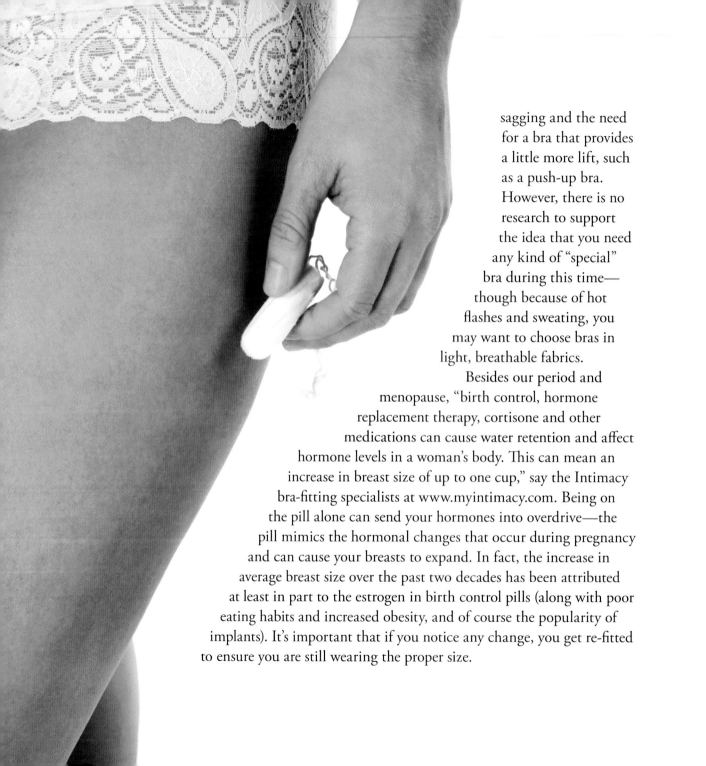

sagging and the need for a bra that provides a little more lift, such as a push-up bra. However, there is no research to support the idea that you need any kind of "special" bra during this time—though because of hot flashes and sweating, you may want to choose bras in light, breathable fabrics.

Besides our period and menopause, "birth control, hormone replacement therapy, cortisone and other medications can cause water retention and affect hormone levels in a woman's body. This can mean an increase in breast size of up to one cup," say the Intimacy bra-fitting specialists at www.myintimacy.com. Being on the pill alone can send your hormones into overdrive—the pill mimics the hormonal changes that occur during pregnancy and can cause your breasts to expand. In fact, the increase in average breast size over the past two decades has been attributed at least in part to the estrogen in birth control pills (along with poor eating habits and increased obesity, and of course the popularity of implants). It's important that if you notice any change, you get re-fitted to ensure you are still wearing the proper size.

AGING

Just like our faces, our breasts can show our age. It's safe to assume that all women know aging has adverse effects on their breasts. Gravity is perhaps the worst culprit. Paired with the loss of skin elasticity that comes with age, gravity makes sagging over time inevitable. Add to that the body changes most women experience during their lives—pregnancy, weight loss and gain, etc.—and it's clear that the breasts take quite a beating! As a result, they can end up not just sitting lower, but actually changing shape and size entirely.

Unfortunately, there has been no solid evidence that suggests you can do anything

to prevent sagging. Some people say sleeping in your bra or constantly wearing an underwire will help, but others argue that wearing a bra *causes* sagging, because

> ## Your Bra and Your Body Tit-Bit
>
> There are some handy dandy gadgets on the market that can help combat the effects of aging. Try Bralief or Fashion Forms' Strap-Mate, both of which help boost the lift your bra provides by pulling the straps together in the back. Not only will this make your breasts appear younger and perkier, it will also keep pesky straps from falling down.

our breasts are made up of ligaments and those ligaments aren't able to retain their strength when a bra is doing their job for them. (We'll be exploring these ideas more in-depth in Chapter 6.)

But once your girls begin to head south, you don't have to go under the knife—the right bra can turn back the hands of time. Simply finding a bra that fits correctly can take years and pounds off your appearance by boosting your breasts back up to their proper position. If you'd like some added oomph, you can always opt for a push-up bra or a bra with some padding. Many women think they are "too old" for a push-up bra, but this is not the case! The only number you should pay attention to when it comes to your bra choice is your band size. You have a right to perkier breasts at any age!

It's time to separate the myths from the facts! Is your bra bad for your health? Can it cause cancer? Continue on to Chapter 6 to find out more.

six

Breast Rx

C<small>AN YOUR BRA BE BAD FOR YOUR HEALTH</small>? A<small>LL YOU HAVE TO DO IS</small> G<small>OOGLE</small> the words "bra" and "cancer" and thousands of posts will pop up. Believe it or not, there is a debate about whether your bra can *cause* cancer. The subject has even been studied and researched.

As you'll learn in this chapter, that's not the only health concern surrounding bras. The wrong bra can cause problems both inside and out—everything from bad posture and skin irritations to muscle strain, migraines, and even indigestion! Your bra can even negatively affect your ability to *breathe* properly. And besides affecting how we *feel*, the wrong bra can also affect how we *look*—not just temporarily but, some say, permanently.

There's a lot of disagreement out there about bras' impact on our health. There are people who believe underwire harms ultra-sensitive breast tissue; others think it's necessary for proper support. There are some who say wearing a bra contributes to sagging breasts, and others who believe a bra helps *prevent* sagging. As you continue reading this chapter, you'll learn what's true and what's not, and how to separate bra myths from the bra facts.

STRAIN

As if stress and everyday life don't put enough strain on our bodies, we have to worry about our bras doing it, too! The one thing that everyone seems to agree on is that an improperly fitted bra can cause muscle strain. If you're feeling tension in your shoulders, upper back, neck, and head, your bra could be to blame—it may not be giving you the support you need. And when you experience upper body strain, it affects your ability to stand up straight, causing poor posture. Fuller-breasted women carry even more weight on their shoulders (literally), so getting a fit that prevents strain is that much more important.

Too-tight straps and back bands can also cause another problem: headaches. "If [your bra] is too tight around the back, it can compress the muscles of the upper back, which will then compress a nerve going up toward the scalp, triggering tension and headaches," says Dr. Dave E. David, a Massachusetts-based OB/GYN.

These problems can be seen as well as felt. If your bra is leaving any kind of marks, either around your ribcage or on your shoulders, it's putting a strain on your body (not to mention irritating your skin). As we mentioned in Chapter 3, you'll want to make sure you can fit at least one to two fingers underneath your band at all times. And to reduce pressure on your shoulders and the potential for strain, you can opt for wider straps (at least a half-inch in width) and bras with underwire that offer more support in the cups.

Bras can also put strain on your lungs. Believe it or not, a bra that's too tight can affect your ability to *breathe*! Patricia Bowden-Luccardi is a breathing therapist and educator for the Radiance Wellness Center in Hudson, New York, and lecturer on "The Power of Breath" at Massachusetts' Canyon Ranch Resort and Spa. "When your bra is too tight, it inhibits proper breathing," says Luccardi. "And when your breathing is constricted, scientific evidence links that to cardiovascular disease, high blood pressure, and other symptoms like gas, bloating, and acid reflux." The website Optimal Breathing (www.breathing.com) makes the analogy that trying to breathe deeply when your chest and back muscles are restricted by tight-fitting clothing (like a too-tight bra) is like "trying to blow up a 5-quart balloon inside a 3- to 4-quart bottle." A better-fitting bra will not just make you look and feel better, it will help you breathe a little easier, too.

113

Are There Ways to Increase Breast Size "Naturally"?

· ·

We've all seen the infomercials about exercise, massage, creams, and "herbal supplements," and heard the middle-school exercise myths ("we must, we must, we must increase our busts!"). But short of hormones or gaining weight, can we really increase the size of our breasts? In short, no. Weight training can strengthen the underlying chest muscles, but that won't necessarily make breasts larger. As for herbal supplements, there is no medical evidence to support the claims that these really work.

An external "tissue expander" system known as Brava (www.mybrava.com) has shown promising results in some women. The company claims women who follow the regimen can boost their breasts by as much as a full cup size. The regimen? Wearing a battery-powered, vacuum-like bra device (torture device?) eleven hours a day for at least ten consecutive weeks. Ouch!

SICKNESS

It's scary to think that a bra could actually make us sick. But some researchers believe it has the potential to do just that. The controversial 1996 book *Dressed to Kill: The Link Between Breast Cancer and Bras*, by Sydney Ross Singer and Soma Grismaijer, outlined the findings of a study they conducted of nearly 5,000 women in which they claim to have found a link between bras and breast cancer (although it's important to note that no other studies have duplicated the book's findings, so the information in it should be taken with a grain of salt). The authors say they discovered that women who wear tight-fitting bras (bras that are tight enough to put pressure on the lymphatic system, an internal network of vessels and nodes that flush waste from the body) twenty-four hours a day are 125 times more likely to get breast cancer than women who do not wear bras at all, and women who wear bras more than twelve hours a day increase their chances of getting breast cancer dramatically.

Much like tight bras can press against our upper body and restrict our breathing, Singer and Grismaijer say, bras (specifically those with underwire) press against our breast tissue, restricting circulation and

Breast Rx Myth Debunked

Breast cancer is said to be more common in Western cultures where women have been wearing bras for more than a century. This has added fuel to the fiery debate that bras contribute to causing breast cancer. However, the National Research Center for Women and Families says that there are more plausible explanations for this, such as the fact that in less-developed countries, people have less access to medical care and therefore cases of breast cancer often go undiagnosed. Other researchers suggest that a difference in nutrition—like the higher saturated fat content in the Western diet—may better explain the difference. People also tend to not live as long in these areas, and since breast cancer strikes more frequently in older women, these countries' rates would be lower regardless of whether their inhabitants wore bras.

blood flow to the breasts and causing a malfunction of the lymphatic system. When the lymphatic system isn't functioning properly, it cannot drain waste, trapping toxins in our breasts. This causes the toxins to settle in breast tissue and become reabsorbed, causing cancer.

Critics of this book dispute the way the "study" was conducted, stating that (among other issues) additional variables weren't taken into consideration, such as other known risk factors for breast cancer. Debate continues to rage on.

Before you toss your bra, think about this: While almost all American women wear bras, according to the American Cancer Society just one out of every eight of us will be diagnosed with breast cancer at some point in her lifetime. But if you're concerned, you can simply opt to not wear a bra for part of the day (most likely while you're lounging around at home) or switch to a more comfortable, non-binding one altogether, such as a simple cotton bra without an underwire. For most women, the benefits of wearing a bra far outweigh the potential "risks" described in these claims—which is probably why the bra business is still booming, despite the release of Singer and Grismaijer's book more than a decade ago.

Another controversial claim against bras is that those allegedly contaminated with the chemical formaldehyde are giving some women persistent skin rashes and severe discomfort. Formaldehyde is found in many everyday products as a preservative but has been tagged a "probable carcinogen" or cancer-causing agent by the Environmental Protection Agency and is a known allergen. It's also illegal for use in textiles in this country. There have been no definitive answers on whether the bras in question were actually contaminated with formaldehyde or whether formaldehyde was the culprit in the women's illness.

One sickness that *has* been proven to come in part from your bra is mastitis, the inflammation of breast tissues due to obstruction and infection of the milk ducts. Mastitis can occur in breastfeeding women who wear a nursing bra that is too tight and puts pressure on the milk ducts (though mastitis can be caused by other factors as well, such as irregular breastfeeding or sleeping on your tummy for long periods of time). A looser, more comfortable bra with flaps that doesn't press against the area around your nipple is a good option to help prevent bra-induced mastitis. You can also talk to a lactation consultant if you're concerned. And of course, any and all infections should be treated by your doctor.

Your bra can also make your skin sick. A combination of sweat and your bra's fabric rubbing against the breast (especially if the bra doesn't fit right) can cause a mild, itchy fungal infection. According to Manhattan plastic surgeon Dr. Matthew Schulman, "rashes and fungal infections can develop on the skin on and around a woman's breasts if she's not wearing a material that breathes." This is particularly important for larger-breasted women or women who work out (and sweat) in their bras, and hot and

117

humid conditions can make infection more likely, but this kind of skin irritation can happen to anyone. Switching to a natural fiber bra (such as cotton) can help you avoid infection—the fabric will breathe better and so be less likely to cause conditions in which fungus can grow. A hydrocortisone or antifungal cream applied to the skin on and under the breast can help treat a rash if one has already developed, but be sure to also wash your bras in hot water to prevent re-infection.

SAGGING

· ·

Gravity: What was considered a scientific breakthrough when Sir Isaac Newton first discovered it has, three centuries later, become the enemy of women everywhere. Bras are designed to oppose it, by holding our breasts up as the forces of gravity pull them down. But even the best of push-up bras can't stop our gals from sagging over time. So what really causes sagging? And why does it happen to some women earlier than others? Can it be made worse by breastfeeding? By not wearing a bra? By *wearing* a bra?

Some researchers say that wearing a bra can prevent breasts from developing (or strengthening) their own internal support structure, which contributes to sagging. But doctors disagree. "Overall, gravity plays the biggest role in breast sagging," says Las Vegas plastic surgeon Dr. Samir Pancholi. "We've all heard about the ninety-year-old woman who had small, perky breasts when she was younger and now that gravity has gotten a hold of them, they aren't perky anymore."

According to Dr. Matthew Schulman, sagging mainly results from three things: "Loss of skin support or elastin; loss of the internal supporting structure of the breast—known as Cooper's ligaments—

which serve as an 'internal bra'; and involution or loss of breast tissue with age, weight changes, and pregnancy."

Pancholi elaborates on the factors that contribute to sagging:

Pregnancy. "As the breasts increase in size, the skin stretches. Many times, the skin will stretch farther than its elastic fibers can handle. When this happens, it's like a rubber band that has been stretched out for too long—it simply won't spring back."

Aging. "As women age, the different elements of the environment [affect] the integrity of the skin. This causes the skin's structural components to

break down and allows it to stretch, causing sagging."

Augmentation. "When women come in for surgery to enlarge their breasts, the bigger the implant, the more the skin gets stretched out, and it's like the rubber band effect all over again. These elastic fibers can only hang on for so long before they allow the breasts to start sagging. This is compounded by implants that are placed above the muscle as opposed to underneath it. [An implant placed above the muscle] only has the skin and breast tissue to keep it in place—pretty stretchy tissue and not the strongest elements of the body."

120

Breast Rx Myth Debunked

Does sleeping in a bra help prevent sagging? Doctors say there is no evidence to support such claims. Just sleep in whatever makes you feel most comfortable!

Does Breastfeeding Cause Sagging?

· ·

While pregnancy surely contributes to breast sagging, a 2007 study dispels the myth that *breastfeeding* alone does. The American Academy of Plastic Surgeons found that while 55 percent of women studied noticed an adverse change in the shape of their breasts following pregnancy, none reported any changes after breastfeeding for a duration of two to twenty-five months. The same study also found that it wasn't the swift weight gain and loss associated with pregnancy that determined whether a woman's breasts sagged. Instead, it was factors like the woman's pre-pregnancy BMI or body mass index, the number of pregnancies she'd had, whether or not she had large breasts before pregnancy, her age, and whether or not she was a smoker.

Is Underwire Doing Us More Harm Than Good?

· ·

There has been a debate over potential "harmful" effects of underwire in bras for decades. In fact, according to an essay on www.bigbra.com, in two books (one written in 2002 called *Women's Bodies, Women's Wisdom*, and one in 1999 called *What Your Doctor May Not Tell You About Premenopause*) women are encouraged to stop wearing underwire bras altogether. Both cite the circulation of blood and lymph fluid around the breasts and surrounding tissue, stating that underwire puts pressure on these glands, preventing the draining of toxins from the breast.

As logical as it may sound, there has been no evidence to actually support that wearing an underwire bra is harmful—short of being a little painful if your cup size is too small (if your underwire sits in the middle of your breast instead of in the fold, it can pinch the breast tissue). If the underwire is so tight against your skin that it causes sweating underneath or so loose that it shifts and rubs, it could potentially cause or worsen skin irritations, so be conscious of that. Otherwise, go ahead and push those puppies up!

Schulman states that there is no scientific evidence that bras have any bearing at all on whether our breasts sag. In fact, Pancholi says, if anything bras can help in our battle against sagging. "Bras play a huge role in *preventing* sagging. The more support breasts have, the less role gravity plays over time."

Breast sagging is inevitable for most women, except for those with very small breasts. For women with large breasts, it could happen sooner for you because you have more weight pulling the breasts downward. But genetics can also play a part. "Some women simply tend to develop more sagging than others do, which is simply hereditary," says Orange County, California, plastic surgeon Dr. John Di Saia. Di Saia points to weight fluctuation as a factor as well: "Extreme weight loss or gain over time can also speed up [the sagging] process."

Breast Rx Myth Debunked

Can exercising your chest muscles help prevent sagging? Unfortunately, no. Since our breasts are made up of tissue and ligaments (not muscle), there is really no way working out will help keep them firm and in place.

123

As for solutions to sagging, most experts feel that, short of surgery, the only way to prevent at least the appearance of droopiness is a good underwire push-up bra.

Now that we've separated the myths from the facts, let's focus on faux pas. There are plenty of them out there when it comes to bras. Want to keep your faux pas under wraps? Read on to find out how!

seven

Bra Faux Pas

Faux pas: a false step; a mistake or wrong measure.

—Webster's Revised Unabridged Dictionary

WE'VE ALL HEARD THE TERM "FASHION FAUX PAS." THEY HAPPEN ALL THE time. Whether it's a see-through dress donned by a celebrity on the red carpet, or a woman who simply wears an outfit that's inappropriate for the office, faux pas, or fashion mistakes, whether accidental or not, are something we often live to regret.

But when it comes to bras, what constitutes a faux pas, and how can they be avoided? Is it a strap slipping out from underneath a blouse? Is it a white bra that's glaringly obvious underneath a white top? Or perhaps it's a nipple that's popping *through* your blouse, for the entire world to see?

Celebrities know all about bra faux pas. The list of famous fashion "oops" moments involving improperly fitting undergarments (or lack thereof) is endless. Actress Tara Reid inadvertently exposed her breast while on the red carpet in 2004. In addition to her infamous pantyless peek-a-boo moment, singer Britney Spears has had many a nipple-slip, during dance rehearsals, nights out on the town, and even reportedly at a concert in 2007. Janet Jackson introduced the term "wardrobe malfunction" to the world and showed a lot more than she planned during the Super Bowl halftime show on national television in 2004, when her breast suddenly flashed across the screen and stunned the nation. Lindsay Lohan has been photographed spilling out of her top on several occasions. And it's been happening for decades—actress Jayne Mansfield reportedly exposed her breasts *intentionally* on several occasions as a way to garner publicity in the 1950s.

Whether you call it a wardrobe malfunction or simply a nipple slip-up, these are all, for the most part, instances of a woman wearing the wrong bra (although Jackson's incident is still up for debate). And as these incidents show, this kind of thing happens to the best of us—even those with million-dollar paychecks and personal stylists.

So what can you do to avert your own "wardrobe malfunctions" when it comes to bras? This chapter outlines ten common "bra pas" and how to make sure they don't happen to you. Consider these your ten commandments. If you follow them, your bra faux pas will be a thing of the past.

Faux Pas #1: Slippery Straps

Problem: Your bra straps keep slipping down your shoulders or peeking out from under your tops, especially sleeveless, halter, and boat neck shirts and dresses.

"Ugly Bra Strap Syndrome is a condition that affects women around the country who let their dingy, discolored bra straps peek through their clothing," says Bra Straps.com (www.brastraps.com) spokesperson Michelle Soudry. "Women need to realize that bra straps have an expiration date and exposing discolored or worn straps underneath a sleeveless tank is a major don't!"

Straps have long been banished to underneath blouses—or replaced, with the "invisible" clear plastic version. They don't have to be—Bra Straps.com says it's OK to let your straps show when they perfectly match or coordinate with your top (it even has a color guide so you can do

just that). "We like to think of bra straps as an extension of your fashion closet," says Soudry. "Straps essentially become a part of your outfit, for better or for worse."

Still, if you don't want your straps to show, what can you do?

Solution: First and foremost, you can simply opt for a strapless bra, or try the aforementioned clear plastic bra straps, which can be attached to any bra that has removable straps. These are available from Fashion Forms and other bra accessory companies. Many convertible bras even come with a set of clear plastic straps for exactly this purpose.

Another alternative is to apply some double-sided tape between the straps and shirt fabric to keep them in place and in line with your top, or to use a product like Fashion Forms' Strap Tamers, which clip on to your clothes to keep slipping straps

Bra Faux Pas Fast Fact

According to a survey in the UK by Wonderbra, having visible bra straps is one of the worst fashion faux pas you can make. In fact, a third of women surveyed said it looks "cheap" and even men said it's a turn-off! More than half of women said it's the summer's worst style crime and will go to all lengths to avoid it, including tucking straps into their tops, going bra-less altogether, and using bikini tops instead of their bras.

130

at bay. They work for everything from evening gowns to workout wear!

You can also look for a strap connector that links your bra straps in the back and pulls them as far inward as necessary, forming a racerback shape, to keep them out of sight. Strap Connection and Strap-Mate by Fashion Forms are good choices.

And remember, you can always choose to show off those straps (and sex-ify those shoulders) with a decorative pair that acts as an accessory. (The only exception to this is a halter top, which looks best with completely bare shoulders, and therefore should only be worn with a strapless or halter-style bra where the strap is hidden.) Margarita Couture Elite Jewelry Collection offers adjustable straps that clip onto your bra and are made from 140 round Swarovski crystals, for around forty dollars. Or check out www.brastraps.com for all their fun and fashionable choices—the site helps you find the perfect fashion strap for any outfit (even evening dresses and swimwear) and you can even tell on a friend for a strap violation via the Strap Police!

Faux Pas #2: Peek-a-Boo Bra

Problem: Your bra is peeking out above a low neckline or at the arm openings.

Sometimes this is done on purpose—think a blouse only buttoned up halfway in order to display the bra underneath it. But unless you're Madonna, this is tough to pull off. There is a reason why bras are called *under*garments!

If you're daring and it's the right occasion, though, you might be able to let your bra *slightly* peek-through. It can be sexy if it's done *tastefully*. But sexy can turn skanky super fast if you attempt a peek-a-boo bra for an inappropriate occasion. It's NEVER appropriate for the office, the PTA meeting, or anywhere else there are impressionable or influential people around.

Solution: If you don't want your bra to inadvertently show, use double-sided tape to adhere it to your top in places where it could pop out. If you plan to wear a button-down shirt with a few buttons undone or another low-cut top, add a camisole underneath. And if you do want your bra to tastefully peek out (say, on an evening out), then make sure it's a beautiful lace one.

Faux Pas #3: Show-Through Bra

Problem: You can see the outline (and/or color) of your bra through your top.

Sure, sometimes you might want this to happen, like on a night out when it's part of your outfit. Usually, though, when others are able to spy your bra through your shirt, it isn't an intentional fashion choice. Wearing a dark-colored bra under a light-colored or thin top often results in this kind of a see-through situation, but the most common culprit is wearing a white bra under a white top. Logic tells you that white goes under white, but it doesn't actually work that way. And while we attest in this book that nude goes with nearly everything, the most important part is that "nearly"—there are cases in which even nude is noticeable. A very sheer black sweater, for example, or one that has an open knit, frequently displays the outline of a nude bra.

Solution: Invest in nude bras and a couple of black ones (for those sheer black tops mentioned above). To be perfectly honest, including white bras in your rotation is completely optional. Nude bras will remain fairly inconspicuous under nearly everything in your closet, whereas white ones will often show through. When you're dealing with a sheer top or dress, whether it's white, purple, or green, for the most part a nude bra is your best bet.

Faux Pas #4: Uniboob

Problem: Your breasts are being flattened to your chest, creating the appearance of a single mass, or "uniboob."

This is a common issue when wearing compression-style sports bras that do not have separate cups, but it can also occur when your top or dress is too tight in the chest.

Solution: If your sports bra is to blame, the best option here is to simply switch to an encapsulation-style that supports the breasts separately.

In the case of a too-tight dress or top, obviously the best option is to switch to a dress that fits well up top! But if you can't, try switching to a front-closure bra that will pull your breasts inward or adding inserts, like cutlets, that will help boost your breasts up. The cleavage created will dispel the uniboob illusion.

Faux Pas #5: Double-Bubble Booby

Problem: Your breasts are being squished in a way that creates the illusion of four boobs, or a "double-bubble," beneath your clothes.

Usually this happens when your bra is too tight, which squeezes your breast tissue up and out over the top of the cup.

Solution: Go get fitted, and make sure you aren't wearing a cup size that's too small! Another potential solution: Try a fuller-coverage bra, which will encase more of your breast tissue in the cup and leave less to bulge out of the top!

Faux Pas #6: Bra Bulge

Problem: Your breast tissue or other flesh is bulging around your bra's cups or band and is visible under or above clothing.

No one wants back bulges rippling through their sheer shirts or breast tissue billowing out underneath their underarms. Not only does this ruin the line of your clothes and create the appearance of extra weight; depending on what's causing it, it can also be uncomfortable for you.

Solution: A too-tight bra is often to blame here, so loosening your bra band a notch could help. In the case of side bulge, try switching to a front-close bra that pulls your breasts inward. This should help keep spillage to a minimum. In the case of back bulge, if loosening your bra doesn't help, you may need an entirely different garment altogether—one that firms and smoothes the back area. I like Sassybax by Amanda

Left: Without Sassybax
Right: With Sassybax

Kennedy, a silhouette smoothing bra/ camisole with no underwire (the support comes from a blend of microfiber nylon and spandex) that's a celebrity favorite. Fashion Forms' Bandeau Bra is also a good option here.

Faux Pas #7: Nipple Poke

Problem: Your nipples are visibly "poking through" your bra and clothing.

This faux pas, also known as visible nipple syndrome, or VNS, occurs frequently enough that the subject has even been studied. Lycra brand asked women in England how they felt about nipple protrusion and a whopping 90 percent of Brits just said no to visible nips. But this can be harder for some women than for others—women with larger nipples may need a little extra help keeping theirs under wraps.

Solution: A lightly padded or lined bra will usually help you avoid showing through thin clothing. But not all dresses or tops accommodate a bra, of course, even with all the options out there. In cases like this, the best thing you can do is cover up those nips with a product like Fashion Forms' Breast Petals that adheres to the skin on and around your nipples and can

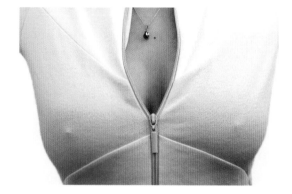

be gently peeled off when you are finished. They're also great for wearing under very sheer or non-padded bras, and work under swimsuits, too.

Another good tip? Always carry a jacket or wrap to make sure you never get cold (the biggest culprit in visible nipples).

Problem: You are boycotting bras, and people can tell!

Women went braless for centuries . . . and in some countries still do. But our better judgment (and advancements in medical science) tells us that there is a reason most women *today* don't leave the house without one on. Letting the ladies hang at all times is not recommended in either the fashion or the medical world. Despite this, a select few still opt to be bra-free.

Sometimes going commando on top is *necessary*, because of the cut of a dress or top. But even if you don't need a bra for support, concealing your nipples is simply more acceptable in society.

Solution: For gals who prefer to go braless (Whoopi Goldberg reportedly did until the age of fifty-one!), there are comfortable options available that cover up

and support without constricting you. You can try the Silicone Adhesive Body Bra by Fashion Forms, which is simply a pair of individual cups that adhere to your breasts, with no straps, band, or underwire to irritate you. They are also virtually invisible under t-shirts or any other item of clothing.

You can also look for a camisole with an attached "shelf bra," which has support built in, or a bralette, which is a comfy first step in the right bra-wearing direction.

Bra-llelujah! by Spanx is an all-hosiery comfort bra that is completely seamless (it's made out of the same material as pantyhose!). It's perfect for easing anti-bra gals into the bra-wearing world.

"People think I'm trying to make a fashion statement because I never wear a bra. It's really that I'm a tomboy at heart."
– Cameron Diaz

Faux Pas #9: Sagging Strapless

Problem: The evening's just begun, and your strapless bra is already heading south.

Most strapless bras use strips of silicone around the band to help it adhere to your skin. But even if you're wearing the right size, sweat, oily skin, or repeated washings can make the silicone stop sticking and start sliding.

Solution: If you don't want to toss a bra that's starting to slip, you can try tightening the band, or switching to a smaller band size (which is generally recommended with strapless bras). It may be a bit uncomfortable, but at least it'll stay up. If that fails, take out your handy-dandy double-sided tape and apply it around the band for added sticking power. And you can also try a backless strapless bra, like Fashion Forms' NuBra, that has self-adhesive cups.

Bra Fashion Fast Fact

Need a little extra oomph in a strapless gown? Insert gel pads, also known as cutlets, into your bra for an added, natural-looking boost.

Faux Pas #10: Too Much Cleavage

Problem: Your low-cut top has left you a little exposed, and everyone's looking at your chest, not your face.

Cleavage is great—when it's the right amount. There is such a thing as "classy cleavage," but the distinction between "classy" and "trashy" can be as little as an inch too much skin. If everyone is staring, chances are you're baring a little too much boob. (*Author's note:* Feel free to skip my advice if you like the attention and the references to Pamela Anderson. I won't be insulted.)

You want to show off your best assets, but without showing it all. First and foremost, listen to your gut when you look in the mirror. If it's telling you you're showing a little too much, you probably are. (Second to my gut is my husband, who has no qualms about telling me to "put those babies back in.")

Keep this in mind as a general rule of thumb—décolletage and the sides of your breasts can be sexy when bared, but if you're in danger of showing areola or nipple, you've gone too far.

Solution: Some bras, like padded or push-up bras, are meant to enhance cleavage, so you may want to avoid those altogether if you fear your dress or top risks showing too much. If your top has a plunging neckline, you can try adding a tissue-thin nude-colored camisole—it'll cover up some of that cleavage without ruining the look of your top.

If you're worried about your top slipping and exposing too much, you also may want to reach for the double-sided tape. Just one piece can mean all the difference between appropriate and too low-cut.

Bra Faux Pas Fast Fact

Double-sided tape deserves a spot in your purse right next to your lipstick, cell phone, and gum. It's handy to always have on hand in case unexpected issues arise. It not only adheres to apparel, but to skin, too, making it the quick-fix item for everything from keeping bra straps in place to hemming a too-long pants leg. Some good choices? Hollywood Fashion Tape, which comes in useful strips, and Dress & Lingerie Tapes by Fashion Forms, which comes in a handy Scotch tape–style dispenser.

Your boyfriend surely notices when you're showing too much cleavage . . . but what else does he notice? Read on to find out more about your bras and your beau!

eight

Bras and Your

Beau

"In the last couple of weeks, I have seen the ads for the Wonderbra. Is that really a problem in this country? Men not paying enough attention to women's breasts?"
—Jay Leno

FROM HIS CHILDHOOD DAYS SEEING HIS MOM'S BRAS HANGING TO DRY ON the bathroom shower rod to the first time he unhooked a bra, and from "bra-strap snapping" in middle school to his first time shopping for his wife or girlfriend's lacy underthings, bras have played a big part in his life, too!

It's no wonder men are fascinated with (and perhaps a little afraid of) bras—and have been since, well, as long as anyone can remember. Maybe it's all those complicated sizes, or the intricate confections of lace and satin themselves. Perhaps it's just what's underneath them. Or could it be that men just want what they don't have? The "mansiere" became part of pop culture when Kramer and Frank Costanza created the aptly-titled "bra for men" on the hit television show *Seinfeld*, and in 2008 Reuters reported that a "bra for boys" had become the hottest selling men's underwear item on a Japanese website.

146

But it's probably safe to say that most men are more interested in the bras the women they're with are wearing than anything that's out there on the market for them. Or as one friend put it, they like their women's bras best when they are "on the floor"! A 2003 study by bra retailer Maidenform seems to support the notion that men base their lingerie choices for women primarily on sex appeal: When buying their partners lingerie, 54 percent said they think of what *they* like first, over what their partners might like.

So here's the burning question: What *do* men like? What does he really want to see when he undresses you? White and lacy . . . or red and racy? What does he notice about your lingerie? (It's usually *not* whether your bra and panties match.) British lingerie site BeCheeky.com claims that studies show red is the color men find most striking on a woman. The fact that sales of red lingerie seem to soar around holidays like Christmas and Valentine's Day only seems to support this—although, red is a popular color for all purchases those times of year.

Color and fabric preferences may vary, but there's one thing men all have in common: they definitely like when your bra is doing its job! It's a proven fact that a well-fitting bra can make you more attractive to the opposite sex, since you'll look more proportioned and your breasts will be pushed up where they should be.

So how can we figure out what men really like? When we're out there looking for sexy duds, how do we know what's going to appeal to a man's eye? Well, by asking the men themselves! We consulted several guys from all walks of life. Here is *The Bra Book*'s man's-eye view on what's best when it comes to bras!

Marc Weiss, a.k.a. DJ CHEF, "The Chef That Rocks"
Celebrity Chef and Television Star
Long Island, New York
www.djchef.com

"I have always thought bustiers were very sexy. There's something very classically sexy about them. Maybe they have that Marilyn Monroe thing going on, I'm not sure exactly what it is, but they have a timeless elegance and sex appeal that I have always liked. If you want to make your bras more attractive to your man, I would say just make sure they're the right size and fit well. (OK, so I watch *What Not to Wear* every once in a while.)"

Will Kaye, a.k.a. "Brimstone"
Professional Wrestler, Actor, and Author
Long Island, New York
www.entrancetohell.com

"I can appreciate the way a quality demi bra accentuates the shape of a woman's 'assets' without being overly confining. I love to see a woman in 'cutesy'-style bras, whether they have bows, gems, flowers . . . whatever is clever when it comes to accenting the various shapes and sizes of a woman's chest. Personally, I couldn't care less if a woman is wearing a matching 'bra and panty' set; I think that's more of a woman's preference rather than a man's. Men for the most part are concentrating more on what's hidden underneath! A self-confident woman like my wife is a serious turn-on for me and when matched with something small and lacy . . . it takes things to a whole new level. Most importantly, nothing compares to a woman who is secure in her own skin . . . the enticing garments are just an exciting extra! Let's face it . . . it's a woman's world and men are just lucky to live in it!"

Pablo Solomon
Internationally Known Artist
Austin, Texas
www.pablosolomon.com

"My wife Beverly was a model. She has always worn and collected sexy lingerie. The bras that I like the best on her are the demi-cup lifting types and the French sets with intricate brocade. Any woman can add many degrees of sensual heat to a relationship with the right lingerie. Careful selection of lingerie can hide flaws and enhance her best features. George Bernard Shaw once said that sex is a matter of lighting. I would add that it is also a matter of mood-setting lingerie."

149

Bras and Your Beau Fast Fact

File this under "only a man could have thought of this." A website called Mrbra.com (www.mrbra.com) not only painstakingly details the bra sizes of nearly every Hollywood actress past and present but also contains a man's view of what the cup sizes really mean. For example, according to Mr. Bra an A-cup means "almost boobs," while a D-cup means "dang!"

Ken Vrana
President and CEO of 1in8 Motorsports and the
1in8 Foundation for Breast Cancer Research
Raleigh, North Carolina
www.1in8foundation.org

"Considering that I own what was recently called the 'fastest growing breast cancer charity in the world,' I tend to spend more time trying to save women's breasts than looking at them. And as a professional photographer who's photographed over 3,000 women, I prefer a woman without a bra at all. But if she's going to wear one I prefer something that creates a lot of cleavage. I also like sports bras, which would, I guess, seem to be a contradiction. Personally, I prefer bras made of soft material, even jersey, rather than stiff bras with a lot of lace on them."

Bras and Your Beau Fast Fact

Men may not like busty gals best after all. According to a survey by PARSHIP.com (www.parship.com), a European online matchmaking service, 31 percent of single men would rather not date a woman whose breasts are larger than a D-cup. However, the men did say that the biggest turnoff was "in your face" surgical enhancement to a woman's breasts, not necessarily the breast size itself.

Can a Bra Make a Man Forget About the Future?

As reported in the *Journal of Consumer Research*, a study of forty-two men aged eighteen to twenty-eight by researchers in Belgium asked men to alternately fondle t-shirts and bras. They found that when the men touched the bras, they valued the future less—and the present more. (Watching video of women running in bikinis had the same effect.) The researchers attributed this to an "appetite" system in the brain that influences a person's desire for pleasure. When offered one or the other, the sexy stimuli caused the men to seek more immediate gratification such as a candy bar or a can of soda as opposed to money, which would help them better prepare for the future.

151

Derrick Hayes, "The Encouragement Speaker"
Author and Inspirational Speaker
Columbus, Georgia
www.derrickhayes.com

"I like to see a bra that fits a woman's breasts so that she feels and looks comfortable. The fit is most important and then the style. Lace bras bring excitement to the eye. I also love to see a matching set of bra and panties."

More from Men

· · · · · · · · · · · · · · · · · · · ·

▶ 33 percent of men chose black lingerie for their ladies while just 16 percent chose red.

▶ Only 1 in 10 women reported exchanging their lingerie gift for something else.

▶ To determine their partner's size, 15 percent of men said they'd check her underwear drawer while 20 percent said they'd simply ask her. Only 4 percent said they'd ask a salesperson to help "guess."

Credit: Marks & Spencer survey

TIPS FOR YOUR GUY

So now that we know what men like, it's time to help *your* man understand what *you* like. Unfortunately, studies show, most men usually end up getting it wrong! In 2008 European search engine site Qype (ww.qype.co.uk) asked 10,000 women how their partners fared in buying lingerie for them over the holidays. Eighty-nine percent of women said they were unhappy with the colors chosen for them, with 53 percent specifically citing red as being "cheap and tacky." And 31 percent said their partners bought them a bra that was two sizes too small!

But not all men are clueless in the buying department. A 2002 survey by Marks & Spencer, a British retailer, showed that British men, at least, seem to know their way around the lingerie section. Half of the men surveyed knew their partner's size and 85 percent said the last time they bought lingerie for their ladies, she liked and wore it.

But even in the UK a quarter of the men did reveal they are embarrassed or uncomfortable lingerie shopping and 1 in 5 said they are nervous and confused about the task. How can we help our men shop for lingerie for us, as so many do?

> ### Bras and Your Beau Fast Fact
>
> Men apparently care more about bras than they do about their health—at least in the UK. A 2003 NOP Omnibus survey found that men are almost twice as likely to know their partner's bra size as they are their own blood pressure! The survey showed that half of men questioned knew their partners' bra size, compared to only 20 percent who knew their blood pressure.

BeCheeky.com (www.becheeky.com) was founded for this very reason—to help men purchase lingerie for their ladies; a "gap" they say has been left by retailers and big lingerie stores. BeCheeky.com offers a "Lingerie Buying Guide for Men" that gives him advice on how to determine her size, how to pick items that she will like wearing as much as he will like seeing them on her, and even a special section on how to buy bras for her! Another UK-based site, Brastop.com (www.brastop.com), offers the same type of guide. A London department store also started a program called "Stocking Fellas," which caters to befuddled boyfriends and husbands who simply can't figure the lingerie thing out.

While most men I consulted for this chapter said they'd like to see a "guide to the art of unhooking bras," sorry, guys. The most useful information we can offer men are tips on shopping for their ladies! After all, this could be one of the most romantic things he does in a relationship. Shouldn't it be taken seriously?

Your man isn't a mind reader. Sometimes you just have to tell him what you really want! Believe me; he'll be grateful for the guidance! So be sure to tear out the tips that follow and fill out the cheat sheet to share with him—preferably before the next big holiday!

Do you have a future with the man in your life? While only you and he know the answer to that, you definitely have one with your bra! What does the future hold for bras? Read on to find out!

BRA SHOPPING TIPS FOR GUYS

Tip 1: Don't be afraid to approach the salesperson. For many men, the lingerie store can be a scary place. Navigating aisles and aisles of silk, satin, and lace, with numbers and size configurations more complicated than a calculus class, can be more than just daunting; it can be downright frightening. But that's what the staff is there for, and believe me, they see dozens of men like you come through those doors each and every day. When I worked at Victoria's Secret in college, one of the things we were specifically taught was how to spot an uncomfortable male shopper, make him more comfortable, and help him choose the right item for his significant other.

Tip 2: Don't try to guess her size! Telling the saleswoman, "She's kinda like, um, around your size," likely won't help you figure it out. You actually might want to raid her bra drawer, read the tags, and write down what they say—or, if it's still not clear, throw a couple of them in a bag and bring them with you! The salesperson will then have a better idea of what sizes and styles will suit your partner best.

Tip 3: Buy for her, not you! While most women do like their guy's input, we also want to wear bras and lingerie that make *us* feel pretty. Now is not the time to pressure her into the bra with the cutout nipples that she was so resistant to before. It's also obvious when a man is buying for himself—and that takes away from the specialness of such an intimate gift. It's safest to think "romantic" and not "racy." You want to impress her, not offend her. When in doubt, a bra and panty set is rarely a bad idea—a survey by Uplifted (www.upliftedlingerie.co.uk) showed that 60 percent of women like their lingerie gifts in sets!

Tip 4: Don't go it alone. If you're close to her best friend or sister, you can always consult them for advice. Make a list of their suggestions and bring that list with you to the store . . . or even better, bring her friend or sister, and let them help you pick something out.

Tip 5: Don't forget to keep the receipt in case she wants (or needs) to return or exchange. It's hard to buy for another person, especially when it comes to clothing. This way if it doesn't fit or she doesn't quite like the way the *style* fits her, she can return it. You shouldn't take it as an insult to your manhood; sometimes she just knows what she likes best!

Tip 6: If you're really unsure, why not let *her* choose what she wants and then just provide the cash? But that's only if you've exhausted all other options. She'll be proud of you if you give it a go on your own first!

BRA SHOPPING CHEAT SHEET

My bra size is _____

My measurements are:

    Bust _____

    Waist _____

    Hips _____

.... **(SELECT ONE)** ....

I prefer:
- ○ fuller coverage
- ○ demi cup

I like my bras to:
- ○ minimize my breast size
- ○ maximize my breast size
- ○ give me lots of support

.... **(CIRCLE ONE)** ....

I like padding ..... *or* .... I don't like padding

I like my bras with embellishments ..... *or* .... I like my bras plain

I like matching panties ..... *or* .... I don't really care

My favorite bras are:

Backless
strapless

Strapless

Balconette

Bandeau

Bralette

Bustier/Corset

Convertible

Demi-cup

Front-closure

Full-coverage

Minimizer

Padded

Plunge

Racerback

Sports

T-shirt

Other _____

My favorite bra colors are:

Other _____

My favorite materials are:

 Cotton Lace Satin  Silk   Other _____

I feel sexiest in _____

Don't even bother buying me _____

nine

Bras and Beyond

The Future of Bras

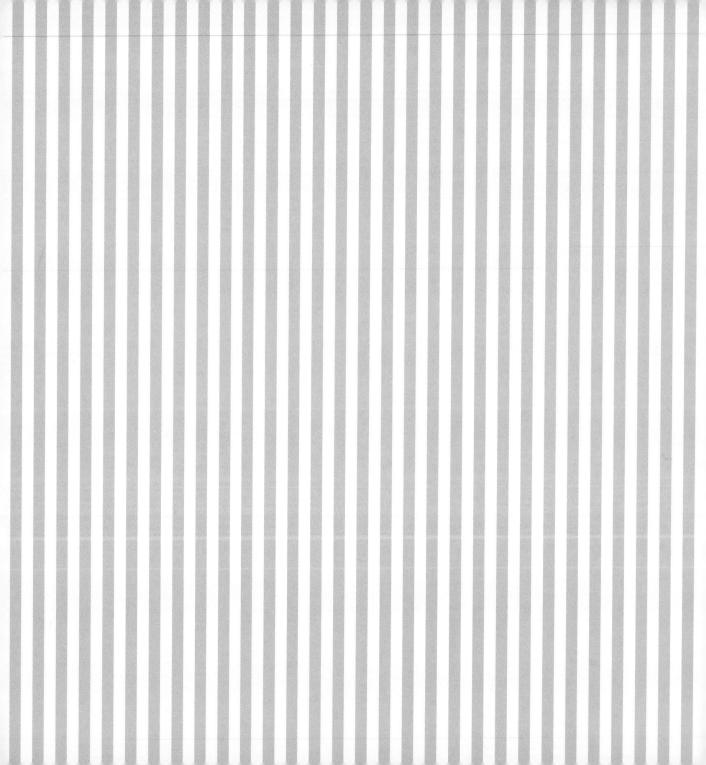

Bras have come a long way since they were introduced in the early 1900s. Materials like Lycra, "push-up" technology, and cup sizes have helped transform bras from a modified corset to the sexy support device we know today.

So what's on the horizon for the next 100 years? Just like in any other industry, new technology is constantly being used to enhance the bra as we know it. Hi-tech fabrics, new support mechanisms, and construction improvements are making the bra even better every day. And now that women everywhere are getting educated about bras, retailers are stepping up with improved service and better-trained salespeople—all to help our bras do the best job they can do. This chapter explores the newest innovations you need to know about—starting with design.

DESIGN AND CONSTRUCTION

Ever wonder how a bra is born? Designing a bra involves some complex engineering. Remember, one piece of fabric that weighs as little as 1.6 ounces has to be able to support and hold all shapes, sizes, and weights of breasts. Not to mention, each new bra that hits the market has to be more innovative than the last. Bra-makers are always striving for better: better support, better comfort, better durability . . . not to mention greater attractiveness to the consumer. Bra-makers also have to keep up with ever-evolving fashions. How do they do it? Mostly, through innovation in design.

THE PROCESS

Usually, design innovation comes from some sort of need in the marketplace. For example, as tops and dresses have gotten more complicated, bra-makers have scrambled to design bras that are convertible in more than just a few ways or bras with the fewest number of "parts" possible. Lower-cut tops and dresses have, of late, prompted a whole new category: convertible bras with a "deep plunge."

Every new bra design begins with a concept—like a bra with an extra-deep plunge—which is conceived and crafted by a bra designer. After a concept is conceived, a technical design is sketched and a pattern is created. From that pattern, a prototype or "working model" is crafted by machines or by hand, or a combination of both, depending on what the design entails. The methods of making a prototype vary from company to company. Often a pair of cups is formed by "hot pressing" foam into the proper shape. Then the other parts, such as the band and straps, are sewed on. This prototype often goes through many incarnations to get the details just right and to make sure every part is not just fashionable, but functional.

Once the prototype is refined, a live "fit model" is brought in. The model tries the prototype on and describes what the bra feels like to wear: where it's comfortable, where the fit feels off. The design is then adjusted if necessary.

After that, the designers, manufacturers, and marketing team collaborate to ensure they have a sellable product that will appeal to as many women as possible. They all want the new bra to be "the next big thing" and, obviously, make a profit.

> ### Bras and Beyond Fast Fact
>
> In 2008, Britain's De Montfort University gave the world's first Ph.D. in Intimate Apparel, for a research project that looked at how adjustments in bra cup design can affect back pain.

One bra that was considered "the next big thing" was the Original Water Bra. When Ann Deal, CEO of Fashion Forms, introduced it in 1997, it was the only bra that credibly mimicked breast implants, giving women who yearned for them a non-surgical alternative. The same was true for the Wonderbra, which was introduced to the U.S. market in the mid 1990s and quickly became a phenomenon.

Tara Cavosie, a bra designer for Fashion Forms, came up with one of the most innovative bra designs ever in 2000 when she created the Backless Strapless

165

> ## Past Innovations in Bra History
>
> Between the 1920s and the 1970s bra company Maidenform pioneered the idea of different cup sizes, patented the adjustable bra strap fastener, and introduced the first maternity bra.

Bra. Now on her fourth new bra design, she's constantly improving on bra-making techniques and staying tuned in to demands in the marketplace. The backless strapless was flying off store shelves, but she found women wanted a style that felt (and looked) a little more like wearing nothing. So she set out to make a virtually "invisible" bra, a new backless strapless called the Bare Uplift. The bra uses an innovative silicone material, similar to the material used in "cutlets," that has never been used in a bra before. It feels like natural breasts and actually stays on and holds up your breasts without straps or a back band.

THE FUTURE

So what does the future hold for bra design? Cavosie says what women really need now is a "fully customizable bra." "Everyone can't go out and buy a custom-made bra. We need a bra that people can customize in their homes, while they're getting ready. With a snap here, a clasp there, the bra would be able to be adjusted in a way that it feels like it was *made* for you." Cavosie has designed just that, and her forthcoming bra for Fashion Forms, called the Formula Bra, is the first of its kind.

What other innovations can we expect to see in the next few years? According to a 2008 *Newsweek* article, to stop sagging sales, bra makers have recently begun to focus more on structural innovations. They cite Maidenform's Breakthrough Backless Bra, which has straps that are lined with silicone and loop around the arm sockets to keep the bra from slipping. Multi-way or convertible bras are another great

Fit Models

The standard fit model for bras is a size 34B. To determine the dimensions for all the other sizes, "They scale up or down from that," says Marla Greene, a New York-based former bra buyer. "For large size/full figure bras, they actually use either a 36C or 38C model. The full figure styles cannot be scaled up from a 34B since it is an entirely different fit, frame, and cup capacity. Each vendor uses different frames and cup capacities and they all vary." Since fit models are only human, it's safe to say that if the model's size is a little "off" (for example, she's not an exact "B"), then the brand's sizes could be a little off, too. Many experts believe this is part of the reason fit varies from brand to brand and even between styles within each brand.

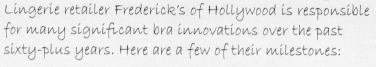

Past Innovations in Bra History

Lingerie retailer Frederick's of Hollywood is responsible for many significant bra innovations over the past sixty-plus years. Here are a few of their milestones:

▶ In 1948 Frederick's debuted what would become the rising star of the bra industry: the world's first push-up bra.

▶ In the 1960s Frederick's introduced the front-hook bra, bras with shoulder pads, padded girdles, and body shapers.

▶ In 1981 the bra got a new companion thanks to Frederick's: the thong!

example. On these bras, straps are made to be detachable, and you can wear them a variety of ways: halter-style, strapless, cross-back, one-shoulder. You can also simply wear it strapless, making it a truly versatile undergarment and replacing the need to own several different specialty bras to accommodate everything in your closet. A recent version has eyelets all along the top of the cups and band so that the straps can be hooked *100* different ways.

Other recent and upcoming innovations in design and construction?

▶ Bras used to be made in pieces and sewn together, creating uncomfortable seams that could sometimes be seen through clothing.

Now, "molded cup" bras are made in one piece so that they are completely smooth and seamless and also keep their shape even when they're not being worn.

▶ New laser cutting techniques have eliminated the need for stitching. Laser cutting prevents fabrics from fraying and allows the bra to lie completely flush with the body, virtually eliminating any visible lines. (The same technology is being used in underwear to eradicate visible panty lines, too.)

▶ Many manufacturers have stopped using tags in an effort to cut down on discomfort. Instead, they stamp size and care info onto the inside of the bra's band.

▶ New bras are also being designed to hide figure flaws. Bra-llelujah! by Spanx and Sassybax's bras, for example, were engineered specifically to hide back fat.

▶ Instead of thick, bulky padding, manufacturers have been experimenting with more natural-looking options. Some bras are now using molded foam "gradual" padding, which is thicker at the bottom of the cup and thins out as it nears the top, offering a boost without the bulky look. For smaller-busted women, Wacoal's Top Solution bras has padding at the top of the cup instead of the bottom to fill in gaps left from lack of volume.

169

The bra industry has also come up with a way to make up for the places where design still falls short. Bra accessories, many of which are discussed in Chapter 7, are another way the bra industry has evolved to meet demand in the marketplace. No bra out there can perfectly meet all our needs but by adding an accessory, we can often get to *almost* perfect.

FABRIC AND MATERIALS

While design is important, improvements in fabrics and materials are just as essential. The first bras were made out of a cotton-based material; then came nylons and satin. Today, there are many more fabric options to choose from, offering benefits from increased durability to better stretch. There are even new fabrics that are better for the environment!

WHY WE LOVE LYCRA

In 1959 Lycra, a stretchy synthetic spandex fiber known for its exceptional elasticity, hit the market, and has since proved to be perhaps the most useful fabric ever invented. Not only has Lycra improved comfort and flexibility, it's also given wearers increased durability—something consumers crave, according to a survey by Lycra commissioned in the UK. It showed that 32 percent of bra-buyers want an "indestructible" bra that can be machine-washed without fading or fraying. Invista, the company that makes Lycra, responded with the introduction of Lycra Black, an elastane fiber that prevents the color from fading in the wash thanks to its spun-dyed technology. It also reduces the "shiny" uneven effect that can occur when dark Lycra is stretched.

breastfeeding women experience as their breasts engorge and deplete.

A More Pleasant Padding

Bra padding used to be made of cloth, until bra manufacturers realized gel and air pockets could provide more comfortable, natural-looking bulk. But the latest padding innovation has been the use of foam, which achieves the same effect without weighing down the bra (or the wearer!).

Foam has also changed the bra industry in other ways. Many bra cups today are lined with thin stretch foam, made of non-allergenic material, rather than fabric. Foam is what allows molded cup bras to retain their shape at all times while maintaining a smooth appearance under tops, and is also thinner than fiberfill lining, so it prevents nipple show-through without adding extra bulk.

When the Mercury's Rising

A fifth of the women in that Lycra survey said they wanted their bras to anticipate their needs by heating up or cooling down as external temperatures changed. While

---

Bras and Beyond Fast Fact

Caterpillar spit, dirt, crude oil, and molten metal are several of the materials that have been used in the making of bras, according to National Geographic Channel special *Secret History of the Bra*.

Unfortunately, while these Lycra bras can withstand more wear and tear than their predecessors and still retain their shape (Lycra can be stretched up to four to seven times its original length and still spring back once released), they still won't stand the test of time when you're talking about repeated washings and wearing. They aren't quite "indestructible" yet!

Lycra has also contributed to recent innovations in nursing bras. Their cups are now frequently made of a stretchy cotton/Lycra blend to allow for the many changes

Can Your Bra Save the Planet?

In 2008 Japanese company Triumph International invented the world's first solar-powered bra. The Solar Power Bra features a solar panel that's worn around the stomach and that creates enough energy to power a small electronic device like a cell phone or an iPod.

This isn't the company's first foray into "environmentally conservative" bras. In 2006 it created a bra that *doubles* as a shopping bag! The No! Shopping Bag Bra (*NO! reji-bukuro bra*) was designed to promote the reduction of plastic bag consumption. When the bra is taken off, it converts into a shopping bag—the extra fabric padding in the cups opens up into a bag that attaches to the bra's underwire. The bra is even made from a polyester fiber that was recycled from plastic bottles.

The same company also previously made three other eco-friendly bras: the Recycle PET Bra in 1997, the Eco-Globe Bra in 2004, and the Warm Biz Bra in 2005.

nothing quite like this has appeared in the marketplace yet, moisture-wicking fabrics, traditionally reserved for exercise apparel, are now making a splash in the everyday bra market because they keep wearers cool and dry. So-called "intelligent fabrics" like Coolmax, Double Dry, PlayDry, and 02Cool (nearly every company has its own patented moisture-wicking fabric) allow these bras to work with the temperature of your body. Most work by pulling perspiration from your skin and then drawing the moisture to the outside of the fabric, where it runs off or evaporates. Microfiber fabrics, usually made of either a nylon or polyester blend, can have a similar "cooling effect" because the fabrics breathe well—they absorb and release perspiration quickly.

Also on the market are hi-tech fabrics that shield us against the elements, adding an extra layer of protection from the sun. Many swimwear and active wear companies are offering clothing pieces with this protective factor, and bras could be next. Apparel company Lands' End makes a Sun Life line that has a UPF (Ultraviolet Protection Factor) of 30 in its active wear, casual wear, and swimwear.

ECO-BRAS

While some bras are being made to keep us cool, others are helping to "cool" the planet. Many of the developments in bra fabrics today mimic what's happening in the world in general: the trend toward being more eco-friendly. Eco-friendly fabrics like those made from highly renewable sources such as bamboo, which is the fastest-growing woody plant on earth, are being used in bras because they are better for the environment. In fact, many bra brands are jumping on the bamboo bandwagon because the renewable grass not only has natural antibacterial properties, but breathes well, too. The same is true for soy-based fabrics. Besides their environmental benefits, both bamboo- and soy-based fabrics offer a cashmere-like softness that is 50 percent more absorbent than cotton.

Other "green" bras?

▶ Pieces from Stella McCartney's lingerie line use organic cotton and natural silk.

▶ French brand g=9.8 uses a fiber made from cultivated pine trees,

173

The Smart Bra

. . . .

If your bra could talk, what would it tell you? While your bra helps support delicate breast tissue, it can't detect abnormalities within that breast tissue. But one day, it may. Researchers at the University of Bolton in England say they are developing what they call a "Smart Bra." The brainy brassiere is said to detect abnormal temperature changes in breast tissue, which is often associated with the forming of cancer cells and tumors as it is indicative of increased blood flow to the area, via a "microwave antennae system" that is woven into the fabric of the bra. When the bra detects what it considers to be a dangerous temperature change, an audible or visual alarm signals.

While the Smart Bra wouldn't replace your yearly mammogram, scientists say it could aid in catching disease early on. However, those developing the bra first have to face the critics, many of whom feel the device won't be sensitive or "specific" enough and could cause anxiety in women for no reason at all. As of early 2009, this bra was only in its prototype stages, but such an undergarment could exist in the near future.

mixed in with some spandex for stretch, in its bras.

▶ Camisoles by Midwest-based brand Urban Fox are made from bamboo and organic cotton blended fabrics that are printed and dyed in-house.

OTHER MATERIAL INNOVATIONS

Innovations are being made in materials for other parts of the bra, too, especially the underwire. In most bras, the metal underwire (made from heavy gauge wire or sheet metal) are wrapped in gel or plastic. While this helps cushion the wearer, underwire can still not only break, but also poke through the fabric of the bra and cause pain. So bra-makers have been on a quest to find alternate materials.

Molded plastic is now being used in place of metal entirely in many bras because of its pliability. In 2000 London-based product design and research company SeymourPowell used automobile machinery to gather data on breast shape and form and develop a molded-plastic piece to replace traditional underwire. The firm identified an "ouch zone" under the arm where underwires frequently dig into bra wearers, and developed "plastic wings" to alleviate this problem. The design of the underwire was modeled after a chicken's two-piece breast bone and replaced twenty-four separate pieces found in traditional underwire bras. While their design made headlines when it was put on the market as the Bioform bra by lingerie retailer Charnos, it was ultimately too expensive to make and in the end fell flat with buyers.

However, the concept of using plastic in place of metal stuck. Instead of rigid pieces of metal with the potential to poke out and cause pain, today's plastic and metal wire-wrapped-plastic underwire is flexible, encased in foam, and stays in place, hidden within the molded piece in a way that reduces the risk of the wire popping out. This new technique is referred to as a "hidden underwire." Hidden underwire also creates a sleeker silhouette and a more comfortable bra altogether. Warner's Elements of Bliss underwire bra features a soft underwire that's wrapped in three layers of fabric for increased comfort.

Straps have also been a recent site of innovation. Some bras now come with straps lined in a material such as silicone that grips the wearer's skin to keep straps from slipping. Another innovation: new gel-strap bras have straps that are infused with silicone gel to disperse pressure more evenly, relieving shoulder strain and preventing straps from digging in.

We've seen what's coming. Now let's talk about some of those breast issues that the bras of the future may help us solve!

ten

Mountains

vs.

Molehills

"In junior high, a boy poured water down my shirt and yelled, 'Now maybe they'll grow.'"
– Pamela Anderson

LET'S FACE IT, EVERYONE HAS PROBLEMS. FOR MANY WOMEN, THEIR biggest problem weighs heavy on their chests—literally. Or perhaps not heavy enough. Whether you feel your breasts are too large or too small, there are problems you face on a regular basis—especially when it comes to bras! Luckily, there are also solutions.

MOUNTAINS

Given the emphasis our culture puts on large breasts, you'd think having them would be easy, right? Not so! The first challenge facing women with larger busts is finding bras large enough to fit. Most retailers only carry up to a DD, and if you are an "odd" size—if you have a band smaller than a 34 but a larger cup—it's even tougher finding your size in stores. Often, online shopping sites offer a larger range of sizes than department stores and chain retailers. But ordering online can be a risky and expensive proposition, since you can't try before you buy.

The website BareNecessities.com (www.barenecessities.com) carries an extensive array of sizes, and there are also bra lines made especially for bustier gals. Dirty Dolls Lingerie (www.dirtydollslingerie.com) has an array of everyday and specialty bras up to a 44DDD, plus a detailed fit guide to help you pick the right size.

Even if the larger-chested woman can find a bra in her size at the department store, she often faces an aesthetic challenge—ugly bras. Lisa Guarini, inventor of the Bra Smart (a bra mold that allows you to air dry your bras while still maintaining their shape) and self-

Dirty Dolls Lingerie

Supporting Mountains: Sports Bras

While even everyday bras are an issue, well-endowed women also have trouble when it comes to sports bras. For some larger-busted women, any form of exercise can be problematic. Many feel the need to wear two sports bras at a time to give them the proper support. While the bra industry is still struggling to come up with the perfect sports bra for the bustier athlete (during a recent trip into a Nike store where even the extra-large sports bra didn't fit me, I learned even sports apparel industry forerunners aren't keeping up with us busty gals), there are some on the market that you can try. The ENELL SPORTS Bra was specifically designed for women who are larger-busted (or are pregnant, nursing, or healing from breast augmentation surgery). It comes in ten sizes and combines the technology of both compression and encapsulation sports bra styles to make the best bra possible for women who need a little more support. Check www.enell.com for ordering options.

proclaimed busty gal, has struggled with finding pretty bras her entire life. "Being a bustier woman, it has always been hard to find the right bras that fit me properly yet were stylish at the same time," says Guarini. Even while working as a bra specialist for lingerie chain Victoria's Secret, she still felt a lack of options.

"Why is it the bras for bustier women always look like granny bras?" she asks.

While you can often find prettier styles for larger sizes online, locating brick and mortar where you can try them on first is another story. Frances Crespo founded her Virginia bra-fitting salon The Full Cup in response to her years of

Could You Be A Mountain and Not Know It?

· ·

While most of us generally know whether we are large- or small-breasted, or somewhere in between, many women confuse the sizing system—especially cup size—with preconceived notions of what those sizes *should* look like. Here's something you should know: When it comes to bra sizes, you are often "smaller" in one measurement and "larger" in the other than you think. Let me explain.

Recently, I had the ladies of Uplifting Makeover host a "bra party" at my house. Out of the fifteen or so women of all ages, shapes, and sizes that were fitted, *every single one* was wearing the wrong bra size. Another thing they all shared? All of the women (including myself) were wearing a band size that was too big—and a cup size that was too small. One woman had been wearing a 38C for years. Her real size? A 30E!

Jo Ann Pasell and Suzanne Gendron, the founders of the Uplifting Makeover, say this is something they see all the time. "Women automatically think a DD and above must be like Pamela Anderson. But it's not! It's all relative to your band size!" While some claim that women's breasts are just bigger these days than they used to be, bra experts say the real explanation for larger cup sizes is that women are simply wearing the right band sizes for the first time!

searching for pretty bras for fuller women like herself. Her store specializes in lingerie for women who wear band sizes 28 through 48 and cup sizes C through K.

"I always strived to buy a comfortable, well-fitting bra," says Crespo. "Among other things, it made a huge difference in how the rest of my clothes fit and how I felt about myself. But it was frustrating. Just because I was a DD—or so I was told for years by people who weren't as trained as my staff at The Full Cup—why couldn't I feel and look as sexy as all the other girls with smaller cup sizes and a wider range of choices in the average American store? Was it too much to ask for a bit of style with that big bra? Did they have to look so . . . utilitarian? I could not understand why it was so difficult to find good bras for the 'fuller-busted woman' like me."

Armed with her family background in the bra industry (her aunt was a bra sample–maker for nearly fifty years), her sewing expertise, and previous business experience, Crespo decided to do something about it, opening up her first store in 2003 (she now has two locations in Virginia).

Larger-breasted women also face more serious challenges. Many opt to undergo breast reduction surgery because their heavy breasts are causing them physical pain. Those who don't can face lifelong back pain and neck and shoulder strain, as well as poor quality of life, because they can't even exercise like everybody else. Women with large breasts can also have to deal with chafing, sweating, rashes, and even fungal infections in the fold of skin beneath the breasts, as described in Chapter 6. Many apply deodorant or powder to the area daily before putting on their bra.

Besides these physical challenges, larger breasts can simply have a tough time "fitting in." It's hard to find clothing that fits properly; either tops fit over the breasts but are baggy around the waist, or they fit at the waist and are too tight across the chest. And lower-cut shirts can be perilous. "Unless you want to have it all hanging out there, your obstacle is 'containing' your breasts," says Tara Cavosie, a bra designer for Fashion Forms who attests she has always been busty. "Especially during pregnancy, a larger-breasted woman will

SPECIAL SIZING FOR MOUNTAINS

Sizing can be confusing when it comes to larger cup sizes. A DD to some retailers can be an E to others. Here is a chart that will help explain sizes for DD and up—but as mentioned in the chart in Chapter 4, sizes can differ, so use this for general guidance only.

Difference Bust Measurement Minus Band Size	US Cup Size
5"	DD/E
6"	DDD/F
7"	G
7.5"	GG
8"	G, H
9"	H, I
10"	H, I, J
11"	HH
11.5" – 13"	I
13" – 15.5"	J
15.5" – 17"	K, JJ

proportioned, but offer extra support as well. Or if you don't want to specifically choose a minimizing bra, you can look for a regular bra that will give you the support you need. Cavosie recommends looking for the following elements:

- Full coverage cups
- Wide shoulder straps
- Underwire
- Back band material that includes stretch
- Only very thin padding or lining

On the flip-side, Cavosie says larger-busted women should avoid the following:

- Plunge or demi bras, which are made to enhance cleavage
- Very thin straps
- Sheer, thin microfiber fabrics

The wrong bra can also make top-heavy women appear heavier than they actually are. As Staci Berner, creator of the Unbelievabra by Shapeez, explained,

186

"I wanted to be the first woman to burn her bra, but it would have taken the fire department four days to put it out."

– Dolly Parton

get even bigger. This is where minimizing comes in."

There are special "minimizing" bras on the market made just for more ample women that not only make you look more

"While I'm not extremely large breasted at a 36C, I do carry the majority of my weight on my upper body. I found that my traditional bras were making me look heavier than I was because the elastic bands were creating unnecessary back bulges and bra overhang, which I was very self conscious of. I searched for bras without the bands but none had the adequate breast support and shaping I needed." So Berner took matters into her own hands and the Unbelievabra was born. "I'm a typical woman who has had two kids, so going braless was not an option for me. The only thing I could do was create the bra of my dreams myself. We appropriately named this new invention the Unbelievabra and started selling them online and to retail stores under the company name of Shapeez. So now, women don't have to sacrifice breast support and shaping to get a totally comfortable, seamless, smooth look from front to back."

While it may be difficult for larger breasted women to find the right bra, once you do, feeling confident is key. "Bras are more than simply a foundation garment," says Guarini. "A bra reflects

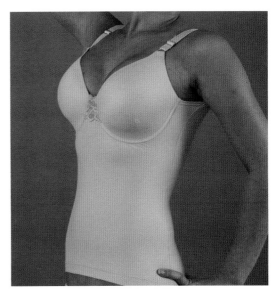

The Unbelievabra by Shapeez

187

everything a woman is and everything she can be . . . fun and flirty, sexy and provocative, strong and supportive. When you are wearing a great bra that gives you perfect support and makes you look good, you feel confident. And just as smaller-sized women are insecure about their chest, so are us larger ladies!"

Speaking of the smaller-busted ladies, they face an array of issues and challenges, too.

The Little Bra Company

MOLEHILLS

· ·

Ask any ample-breasted woman and she'll tell you that women with smaller breasts definitely have it easier. They can fit into almost any top. They don't have issues with exercising and don't have to worry about breast-induced back, neck, or shoulder pain. But in our breast-obsessed culture, many smaller-breasted women go under the knife to attain what their larger-busted counterparts were born with. Those who don't choose surgery rely on their bras to fill out what Mother Nature didn't provide—or at least just fit well. Unfortunately, women with smaller breasts don't seem to have any more luck than women with larger breasts!

Emily Lau, a former television producer, started The Little Bra Company after years of frustrating trips to the lingerie stores. Lau felt that the bras that fit her small frame well looked like training bras, and the sexy ones never fit quite right. "I spent years looking ridiculous wearing ill-fitting bras. That is, until a couple of years ago when I started working with some experts to design the perfect-fitting bra for my petite body type and then tested it out on some friends."

Her yearning to make the most of her assets (without the help of saline or silicone) prompted her to make "the

> ### Enhancing Molehills: Want the Illusion of More Cleavage?
>
> Besides wearing a bra that pushes your breasts up and together, or placing silicone inserts inside your bra to further boost breasts up, you can also dust a little shimmery bronzer between your breasts to add more "depth" to the area.

perfect little bra." Her bras have specially designed "contoured cups" that help create the illusion that smaller-breasted women have more than they actually do. "I find that smaller-breasted women often resign themselves to wearing camisole bras or nothing at all," says Lau. "When I get to personally fit my customers, it's always so exciting to see their reactions. I get hugs and high-fives from women who thought they could never have cleavage.

They tell me that they have never had a bra that fit the way one of mine fits and they love it because it makes them feel pretty!" Some of her bras start in as small as a 28 band size and none are larger than a B cup. Almost all are decorative and fashionable—something she says you don't often find in smaller sizes at other retailers. You can find Lau's bras online at www.herroom.com, www.brasmyth.com, www.barenecessities.com, and at www.thelittlebracompany.com.

Another company, Itty Bitty Bra (www.ittybittybra.com), has a similar mission. It offers pretty, decorative bras in sizes AA through B. Lula Lu, a petite lingerie company based in California, also specializes in hard-to-find smaller bra sizes such as AA and A cups and lingerie that flatters the smaller figure. Even though it calls itself a "petite" lingerie store, the store's founder Ellen Shing says they are not about height (the formal definition of petite in fashion is 5'4" and under), but rather frame and bust size, and have customers who are 6 feet tall.

At a 36A, Shing says she has what is considered to be an "odd" size because

> ### Enhancing Molehills:
> ## Why Demis Are Designed Just for You
>
> Whether you want to increase your size or just be more comfortable, demi cups are a great option for you smaller-breasted ladies because they're designed with you in mind. They have has the least breast coverage but their slightly tilted cups offer a boost by pushing the breasts toward the center for increased cleavage. Demi cups are also designed with shallower/ shorter underwire to prevent poking petite women.

191

of her bigger back and smaller bust. Numerous bra-shopping trips left her discouraged as she couldn't find any of the styles she liked in her size. "It's not that manufacturers don't make 36As, it's just that a lot of the stores either didn't stock them or didn't re-order after they ran out," says Shing. "I then got curious about my other friends' bra shopping experiences, as some of them have even smaller busts than I do. So I asked around and heard all kinds of stories, such as they were often told to go to the children's department even though they were grown women! So, after doing a lot more research, I decided to take the plunge and open up my store and e-commerce site, as it seemed there was a need for this."

Shing eventually launched her own bra line, Lula Lu Petites, because she couldn't find a lot of the styles or fits her customers were asking for in existing lines. Shing's line can be purchased on her website at www.lulalu.com. "I really enjoy what I do, as I feel my store and website help make a lot of small-busted women feel like, 'Ahhh, there *are* bras in my size!' rather than feeling dejected whenever they go to other lingerie stores and leave feeling like there is something wrong with them," she says.

Just like Shing and Lau, Bita Saviss struggled with finding good bras for smaller women; in her case, she wanted a good push-up bra. So she created one herself. "The Lavand Distraction Bra came from my own personal need. I could not find a push-up bra that gave me the maximum cleavage and natural look and feel I was looking for. The gel, water, and silicone bras were too heavy and uncomfortable; the air bras made noise; and other push-up bras just didn't create the full look I was looking for. Also, any bra inserts I tried moved around, and I was always worried that someone might see them or they might pop out! I wanted to create a comfortable and lightweight push-up bra that I could wear all day; a bra that was so amazing that it would make me change my mind about getting breast implants."

Saviss says her bra is the only one on the market that increases breast size by two full cups, and it's comfortable to wear all day. Dubbed the "$88 boob job" by journalists, it's also made in a way that you can choose your breast size increase, anywhere from one to two cups. She offers over eighty bra sizes, in addition to offering specific bra customizations based on individual customers' needs. You can go to www.bitasaviss.com to order.

Another challenge those who are "flat-chested" face is that they may not even register on the size chart in the first place. Bra measurements are calculated based on the assumption that women have an inch or more difference between their band size measurements and their cup size measurements. If you fall into the category of women who don't have that inch, your best option may be to go to the store and try on bras that are closest to your size, then add some cutlets to help fill it out.

MOUNTAINS VS. MOLEHILLS: BUST BUDDIES FACE OFF!

I consulted some friends, both large- and small-busted, and asked them to give me the pros of both! Here are their top ten lists.

Small Breasts: The Pros

1. You don't get back pain.
2. You can wear almost any shirt without the risk of looking "slutty," and you are less likely to be stereotyped in a job interview.
3. You can wear your "true size" in shirts and dresses instead of having to go a size up.
4. You can find a bikini top that doesn't expose a whole boob.
5. Lying on your belly isn't painful.
6. You don't get under-boob sweat.
7. You have less fear of saggy/droopy boobs.
8. You can go braless and still be perky, or add a push-up bra for major cleavage—the best of both worlds!
9. You can wear sexier bras instead of "granny-style" minimizers.
10. Guys always know where your eyes are.

Large Breasts: The Pros

1. They help balance out a curvy figure.
2. They create the illusion of a tiny waist.
3. They give you an excuse to deduct an extra five to ten pounds off what the scale says.
4. You "fill out" your clothes better.
5. You don't have to fear strapless dresses will fall down.
6. No risk of "false advertising." What you see is what you get!
7. You don't need to spend money on cutlets, push-up pads, or anything else—you have cleavage naturally!
8. Small-chested women are usually jealous.
9. You never risk being mistaken for a boy.
10. Men love them!

Loving Your Breasts Just the Way They Are

....

Many of us look in the mirror and see something completely different than what the rest of the world sees, and often so-called "imperfections" (such as breasts that are too large, too small, saggy, or even lopsided) can seem glaringly obvious when in reality someone else wouldn't even notice them.

Body image expert Sarah Maria (www.sarahmaria.com) says society is to blame. "As a society, we have projected certain images of beauty into the world. We then idealize these images and internalize them, believing that we should live up to some external standard of beauty. We attempt to achieve beauty by complying with some ideal, as opposed to connecting with our own inner, innate beauty. When this happens, women suffer."

Using undergarments to mold women's bodies into a desired shape or hide so-called "flaws" is nothing new. The corset of the nineteenth and twentieth centuries created coveted curves by pushing up the breasts and narrowing the waist in order to emphasis womanly breasts, hips, and derriere. And with all the options available to us today, it's easy for us to obsess over our bodies. A thin frame with large breasts is in, sending millions of us not just to the store for expensive bras and accessories, but to the gym—and the plastic surgeon's office.

While it's not always realistic to expect a woman to accept her body just the way it is, there are some steps you can take to at least be more at peace with the way you look. Maria says the first step is identifying exactly what it is that makes you think your body and your breasts are unacceptable. "Learn how to identify these thoughts and detach yourself from them. It's important to realize that thoughts have no truth to them other than the truth *you* give them. Those thoughts that make you feel bad about your body can just be disregarded and discarded."

Website www.myintimacy.com suggests, "Try to cultivate a positive attitude about your breasts and your body in general. Decide to love your breasts as they are. Ideally, your breasts will be your breasts for life. Changing your attitude is entirely in your power."

195

"You know they say beauty comes from the inside, so buy a good bra!"
– Melissa Rivers

The lesson to be learned in this chapter—and in this book—is that good things can come in both large and small packages, and the right bra can help you make the most of whatever package you've got. Bras shouldn't be a crutch, but they can be a tool—a tool you use to make yourself look and feel the best you can, from the inside out!

SHOPPING TIPS

Now that you've read *The Bra Book*, you're ready to go shopping! Here is a compilation of some of the book's top tips that you can take along with you.

1. Choose a store that has a wide selection of bras and *trained* bra fitters on hand.

2. Try to avoid bra shopping during "that time of the month." You can be up to a full cup size bigger when you're on your period!

3. Go to the store armed with a list of what you need and plan to buy: i.e., two nude bras, two black bras, one strapless, one sports bra, one bra without underwire for comfort (this will vary from person to person). Remember: nude goes under *nearly everything*.

4. Be aware of your body type so you know what bras to look for. For example, if you are more of a top-heavy "apple," you likely will be looking for fuller coverage bras, not demi-cups.

5. Wear or bring a thin t-shirt to the store so you can see what each bra looks like under the sheerest of circumstances.

6. At the store, find a bra fitter that you feel comfortable with, and get measured to find your proper size.

7. Be open-minded about your size. If you're surprised (or disappointed), remember that size is just a number (and a letter!). The proper fit of the bra is the most important part.

8. Use your size only as a *guideline*. You will still need to try the bras on!

9. If you're in a bind and there's a bra that you really love but they don't have your size, it's usually OK to go up a band size and down a cup size. For example, if you are a 34DD, try the bra in a 36D and see if it works.

10. Don't be afraid to put the bra on and face yourself in the mirror with a critical eye. If you see any gaps, spillage, digging in, or other signs of poor fit, it's not the right bra. Turn around and look at the back as well. The back band can be very telling too when it comes to proper fit.

11. Don't forget to pick up some bra accessories too, so you avoid any faux pas! Breast petals and double-sided tape are always good to have on hand.

12. Don't get stuck in a size rut. Write down the date of your visit and be sure to plan another one six months to a year later!

CARE TIPS

Your bras are one of—if not *the*—most important articles of clothing
you own. Yet when it comes to care, they often get neglected. In fact,
bras are probably also the most abused, mistreated garments we own. We
throw them in the washing machine unprotected, bend their underwires,
misshape their cups, wear them month after month without replacement,
and then curse them when they're not as comfortable or supportive as they
once were.

Caring properly for your bras is important, but I know we're all busy.
It's not realistic to expect every woman to take the time to hand-wash her
bras. So here are some tips on caring for your bras in a way that will extend
their life and keep you looking forever stylish, *without* cramping your style.

WASHING AND DRYING

We know it's best to hand-wash and soak your bras with either a gentle
detergent like Woolite or a soda-based cleansing wash like Forever New.
In fact, it can make your bra last up to 30 percent longer. But that doesn't
mean the washing machine is the enemy. Some things to keep in mind if
you're machine-washing your bras:

▶ Don't forget to check the tag. If your bra has special washing
   instructions, follow them.

▶ A front-loading washer is ideal; it doesn't have a drum and is therefore
   gentler on your clothes. However, if you don't have one of these, be
   sure to use a netted garment bag (some are made especially for bras)

or a protective casing like the plastic ball-shaped BraBABY. Using something like the BraBABY also helps retain the shape of the bra's cups, which often end up getting crushed. When a bra is tossed in alone, without "protection," a top-loading washing machine can be especially dangerous to straps and bands, as they can "catch" on the drum and get damaged. In the case of an underwire bra, the machine can damage the underwire by bending it or weakening the fabric, causing poke-through, so you'll want to take extra care.

▶ Be sure to first fasten the hooks, so they don't catch on other garments.

▶ Never use bleach, and always use a gentle detergent.

▶ Put the machine on the gentlest cycle possible (most have a "delicate" cycle) and always use cold water. Bras are made from very sensitive fabrics and excessive heat can ruin them.

While machine-washing your bras can work if you're careful, machine-drying is NEVER OK; the heat from the dryer is especially bad for your bras! You should always hang your bras or lay them flat to dry. A good option for helping your bra retain its shape while air-drying is the Bra Smart. You just place your bra into the bra-shaped plastic mold and let it dry with the help of ventilated slits in the plastic. It even comes with a hanger for hanging.

Whatever you do, do not dry clean or iron your bras. Again, exposing your bra to heat is a bad idea!

If you're lucky enough to have a husband who does the laundry, either share these tips or put your bras aside and do them yourself. He may not "get" the importance of taking such care.

Storing

How you store your bras can also have an effect on their longevity. The best way to store bras is to lay them flat in a drawer (unhooked), one right after another. The cups of one bra can sit inside the cups of the next, with tissue paper placed in between. Never fold the cups or shove your bra into or through a too-tight space, as this can permanently damage the cups and underwire.

Packing

Packing your bras for a trip can be especially troublesome. To avoid damaging them while travelling, place softer items like socks inside the cups to help them retain their shape, and nestle them into their own spot in your suitcase, preferably on the side where there aren't any items on top of them.

Another option: Pick up a bra-shaped case, like the Bra Bag from The Brag Company (www.thebragcompany.com). The company that makes the Bra Smart also makes a travel case that keeps your bras from being crushed in your suitcase. You can find it at www.smartbroad.com.

More Tips to Extend the Life of Your Bra

▶ Wash them frequently (if possible, after every use) to remove dirt and oil that accumulate during the day.

▶ If you don't wash your bras after every use, at the very least don't wear the same bra day after day. Instead, rotate between three or four, giving each one a day or two in-between to "rest." Contact with your body heat day after day will cause the bra to stretch and deteriorate faster.

How You Know It's Time to Replace Your Bra

As a rule of thumb, a bra you wear a lot will need to be replaced after approximately six months because of stretching, wear, and tear—a small price to pay for comfort and support! Here are a few indicators that it's time to give your bra the old heave-ho:

▶ You find yourself moving to the tighter hook as time passes, indicating that the fabric is starting to stretch out.

▶ The color starts to fade.

▶ The fabric starts looking worn.

▶ The underwire starts poking out.

Utilize these tips, and you and your bras will have a long and happy life together!

Want More on Bras and *The Bra Book*?

. . . .

Then be sure to visit www.thebrabook.com. The site is chock-full of info you won't find in the book, fun bra facts, tips and tales, Jené's "picks" and where to find them online, plus fun quizzes and more. It's a wealth of bra information that you'll only find online!

Also be sure to look for *The Bra Book* fan page on Facebook at www.thebrabook.com/onfacebook and follow Jené on Twitter at www.twitter.com/thebrabook.

COLOPHON

This book and cover were created in Adobe InDesign by Kit Sweeney. Cover illustrations and most other interior illustrations were drawn by Ralph Voltz. Text was set in Adobe Garamond Pro, with accents in Bradley Hand, Trajan Pro, and Bickham Script Pro. The book was printed by Wai Man Book Binding (China) Ltd.